HELLBOY™

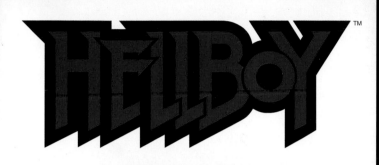

WAKE THE DEVIL

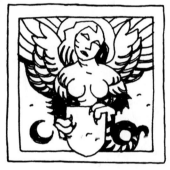

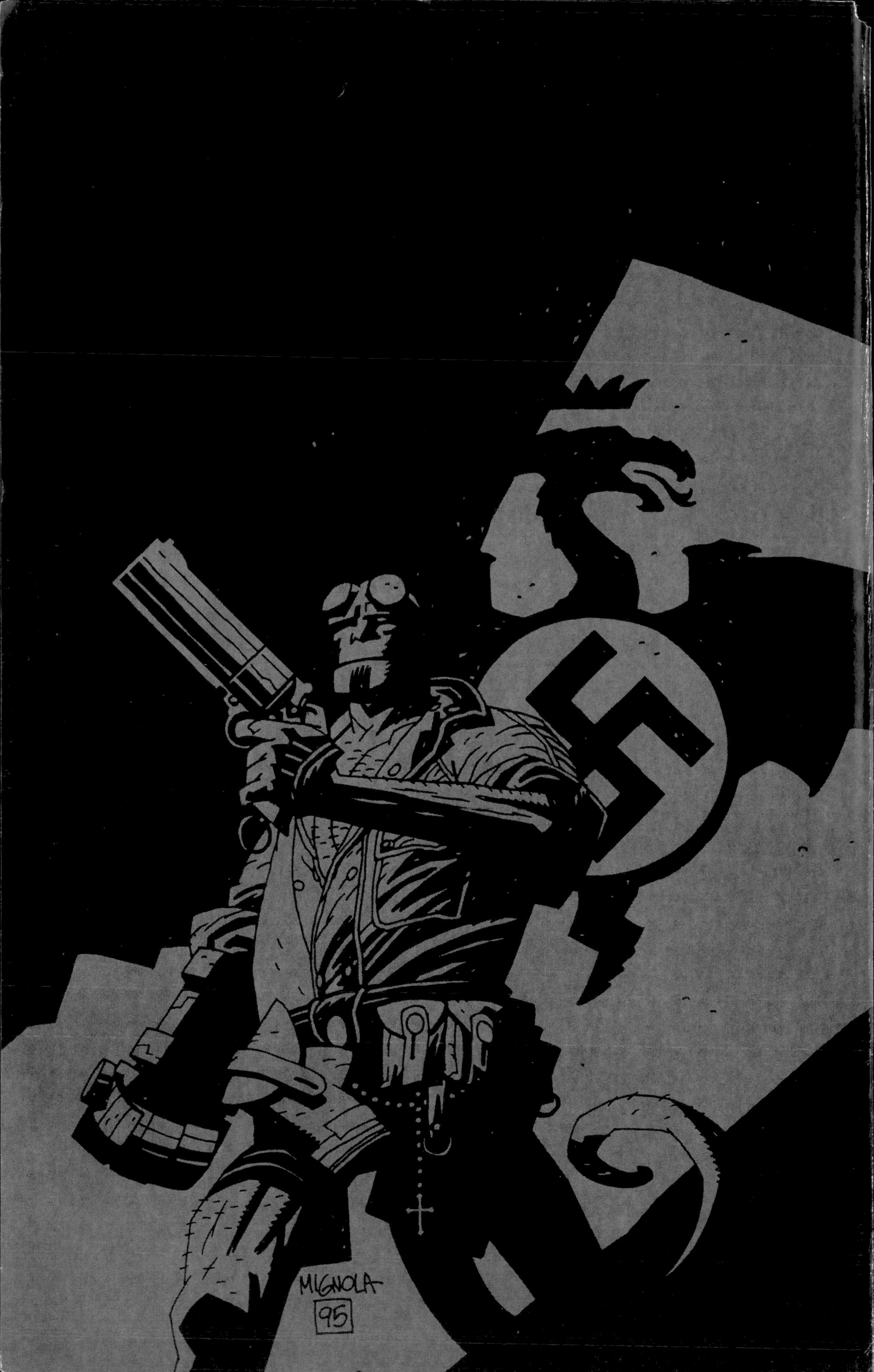
MIGNOLA
95

HELLBOY™

WAKE THE
DEVIL

by
MIKE MIGNOLA

Colored by
JAMES SINCLAIR

Lettered by
PAT BROSSEAU

Cover colors by
DAVE STEWART

✠

Introduction by
ALAN MOORE

Edited by
SCOTT ALLIE

Hellboy logo designed by
KEVIN NOWLAN

Color separations by
DAVE STEWART

Collection designed by
MIKE MIGNOLA & CARY GRAZZINI

Published by
MIKE RICHARDSON

DARK HORSE BOOKS™

NEIL HANKERSON ✠ *executive vice president*

TOM WEDDLE ✠ *vice president of finance*

RANDY STRADLEY ✠ *vice president of publishing*

CHRIS WARNER ✠ *senior books editor*

SARA PERRIN ✠ *vice president of marketing*

MICHAEL MARTENS ✠ *vice president of business development*

ANITA NELSON ✠ *vice president of sales & licensing*

DAVID SCROGGY ✠ *vice president of product development*

DALE LaFOUNTAIN ✠ *vice president of information technology*

DARLENE VOGEL ✠ *director of purchasing*

KEN LIZZI ✠ *general counsel*

Published by Dark Horse Books
A division of Dark Horse Comics, Inc.
10956 SE Main St.
Milwaukie, OR 97222
www.darkhorse.com

First Edition: May 1997
Second Edition: November 2003
ISBN: 978-1-59307-095-3

This volume collects issues one through five
of the Dark Horse comic-book series *Hellboy: Wake the Devil.*

13 15 17 19 20 18 16 14

Printed in China

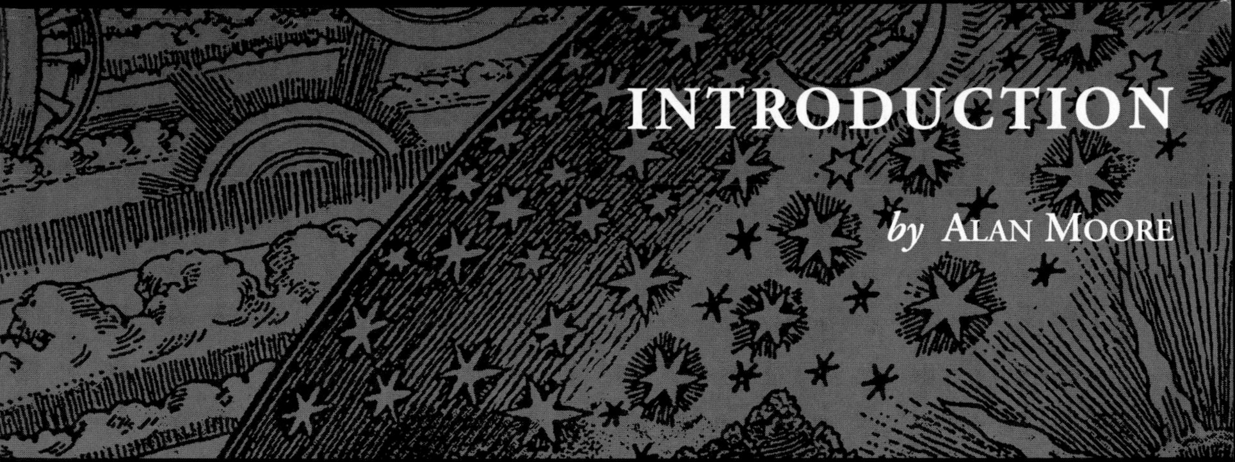

INTRODUCTION

by Alan Moore

THE HISTORY OF COMIC-BOOK CULTURE, MUCH LIKE THE HISTORY OF ANY CULTURE, is something between a treadmill and a conveyer belt: we dutifully trudge along, and the belt carries us with it into one new territory after another. There are dazzlingly bright periods, pelting black squalls, and long stretches of grey, dreary fog, interspersed seemingly at random. The sole condition of our transport is that we cannot halt the belt, and we cannot get off. We move from Golden Age to Silver Age to Silicone Age, and nowhere do we have the opportunity to say, "We like it here. Let's stop." History isn't like that. History is movement, and if you're not riding with it then in all probability you're beneath its wheels.

Lately, however, there seems to be some new scent in the air: a sense of new and different possibilities; new ways for us to interact with History. At this remote end of the twentieth century, while we're further from our past than we have ever been before, there is another way of viewing things in which the past has never been so close. We know much more now of the path that lies behind us, and in greater detail, than we've ever previously known. Our new technology of information makes this knowledge instantly accessible to anybody who can figure-skate across a mouse pad. In a way, we understand more of the past and have a greater access to it than the folk who actually lived there.

In this new perspective, there would seem to be new opportunities for liberating both our culture and ourselves from Time's relentless treadmill. We may not be able to jump off, but we're no longer trapped so thoroughly in our own present movement, with the past a dead, unreachable expanse behind us. From our new and elevated point of view our History becomes a living landscape which our minds are still at liberty to visit, to draw sustenance and inspiration from. In a sense, we can now farm the vast accumulated harvest of the years or centuries behind. Across the cultural spectrum, we see individuals waking up to the potentials and advantages that this affords.

It's happened in popular music, where we no longer see the linear progression of distinct trends that we saw in the fifties, the sixties, the seventies, and so on. Instead, the current music field is a mosiac of styles drawn from points in the past or even points in the imagined future, with no single nineties style predominating. It's happened in the sciences, where mathematicians, for example, find valuable insights into modern theoretical conundrums by examining the long-outmoded Late Victorian passion for the geometric study of rope knots. It's happened in our arts and one could probably make a convincing argument that it has happened in our politics. Without doubt, it has happened in the comics field: the most cursory glance 'round at the most interesting books, whether we're talking about Seth's *Palookaville* or Chris Ware's *Acme Novelty Library* or Michael Allred's *Madman*, will reveal that in even the most contemporary of modern comic books, our previous heritage looms large, and is in many ways the most important signifier. Which brings me to Mike Mignola's *Hellboy*.

Hellboy is a gem, one of considerable size and a surprising lustre. While it is obviously a gem that has been mined from that immeasurably rich seam first excavated by the late Jack Kirby, it is in the skillful cutting and the setting of the stone that we can see Mignola's sharp contemporary sensibilities at work. To label *Hellboy* as a "retro" work would be to drastically misunderstand it: This is a clear and modern voice, not merely some ventriloquial seance-echo from beyond the grave. Mignola, from the evidence contained herein, has accurately understood Jack Kirby as a living force that did not perish with the mortal body. As with any notable creator, the sheer electricity inside the work lives on, is a resource that later artists would be foolish to ignore just because times have changed and trends have fluctuated. Did we stop working in iron and stone the moment that formica was discovered? No. We understood those substances to be still-vital forms of mineral wealth that we could build our future from, if only we'd the wit and the imagination.

Mike Mignola has these qualities in great abundance. *Hellboy*'s slab-black shadows crackle with the glee and enthusiasm of an artist almost drunk with the sheer pleasure of just putting down these lines on paper, of bringing to life these wonderfully flame-lit and titanic situations. Images, ideas, and thinly disguised icons from the rich four-color treasure house of comics history are given a fresh lick of paint and are suddenly revealed as every bit as powerful and evocative upon some primal ten-year-old-child level as when we last saw them. This, perhaps, is *Hellboy*'s greatest and least-obvious accomplishment: the trick, the skill entailed in this delightful necromantic conjuring of things gone by is not, as might be thought, in crafting work as good as the work that inspired it really was, but in the more demanding task of crafting work as good as everyone *remembers* the original as being. This means that the work must be as fresh and as innovative as the work that preceded it seemed at the time. It's not enough to merely reproduce the past. Instead we have to blend it artfully with how we see things now and with our visions for the future if we are to mix a brew as rich, transporting, and bewitching as the potions we remember from the vanished years.

Hellboy is such a potion, strong and effervescent, served up in a foaming beaker from an archetypal Mad Scientist's dungeon or laboratory. The collection in your hands distills all that is best about the comic book into a dark, intoxicating ruby wine. Sit down and knock it back in one, then wait for your reading experience to undergo a mystifying and alarming transformation. *Hellboy* is a passport to a corner of funnybook heaven you may never want to leave. Enter and enjoy.

For Dracula and all those other vampires I have loved.

CHAPTER ONE

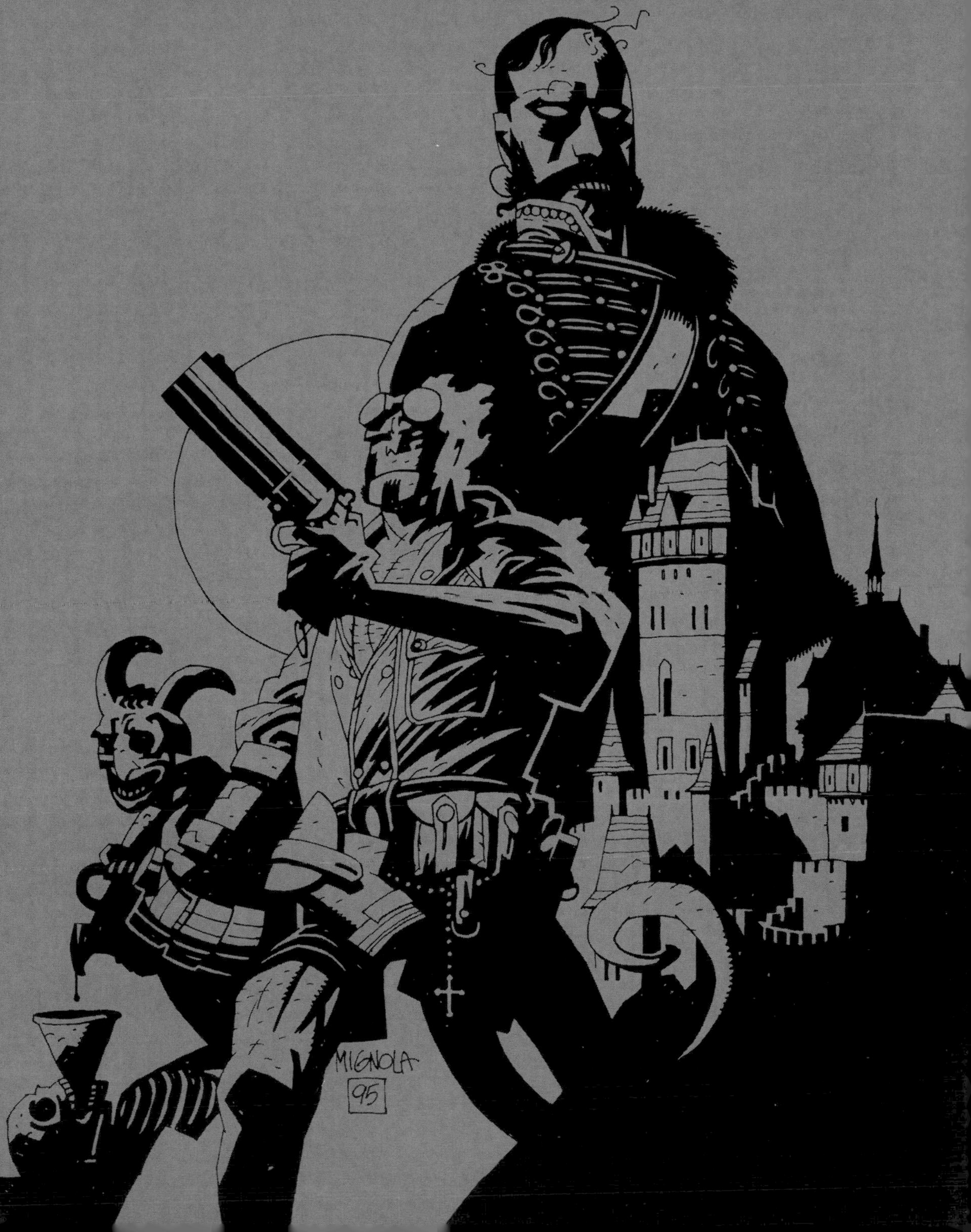
MIGNOLA
95

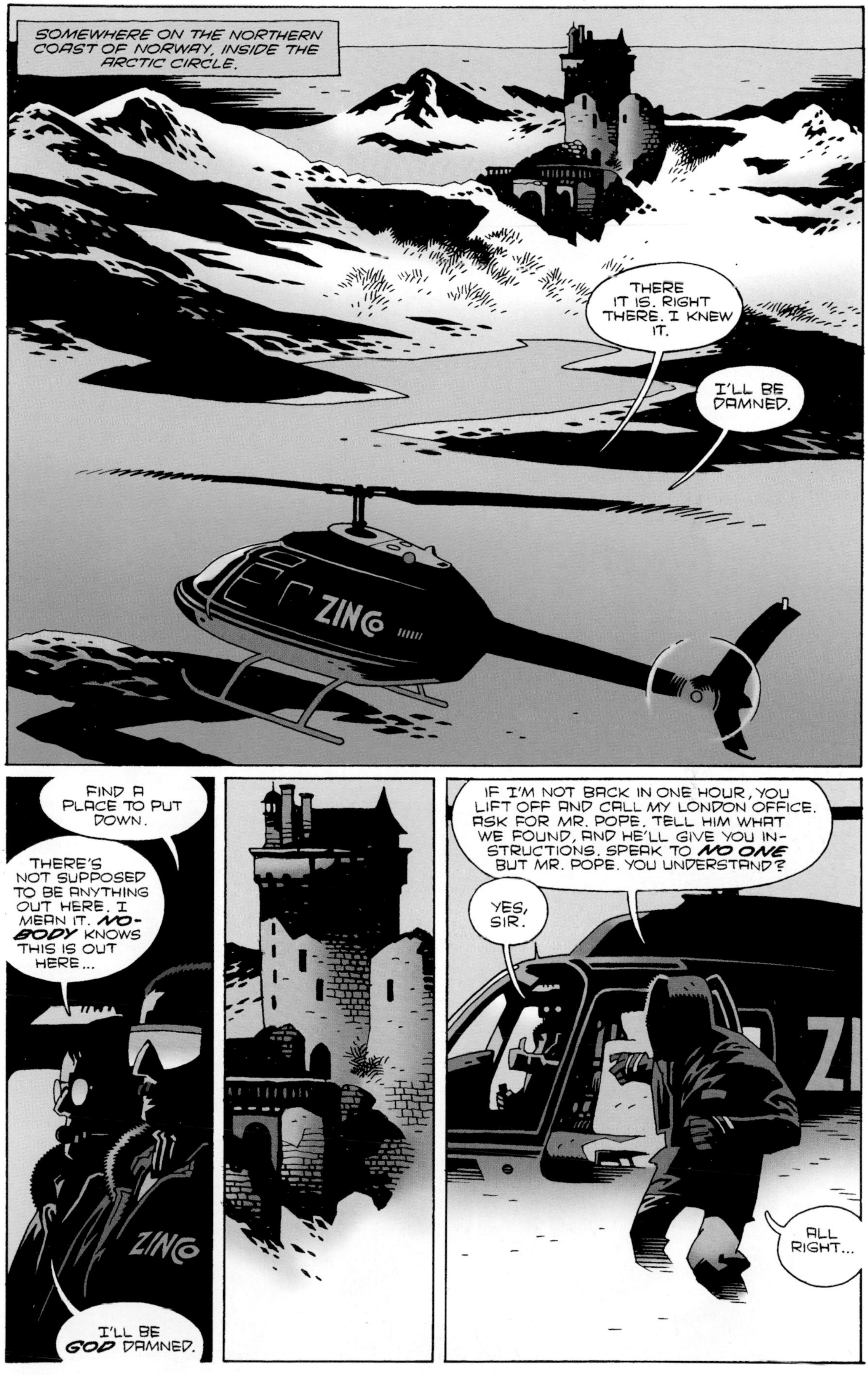
SOMEWHERE ON THE NORTHERN COAST OF NORWAY, INSIDE THE ARCTIC CIRCLE.
THERE IT IS. RIGHT THERE. I KNEW IT.
I'LL BE DAMNED.
ZINCO
FIND A PLACE TO PUT DOWN.
THERE'S NOT SUPPOSED TO BE ANYTHING OUT HERE. I MEAN IT. NO-BODY KNOWS THIS IS OUT HERE...
I'LL BE GOD DAMNED.
IF I'M NOT BACK IN ONE HOUR, YOU LIFT OFF AND CALL MY LONDON OFFICE. ASK FOR MR. POPE. TELL HIM WHAT WE FOUND, AND HE'LL GIVE YOU IN-STRUCTIONS. SPEAK TO NO ONE BUT MR. POPE. YOU UNDERSTAND?
YES, SIR.
ALL RIGHT...

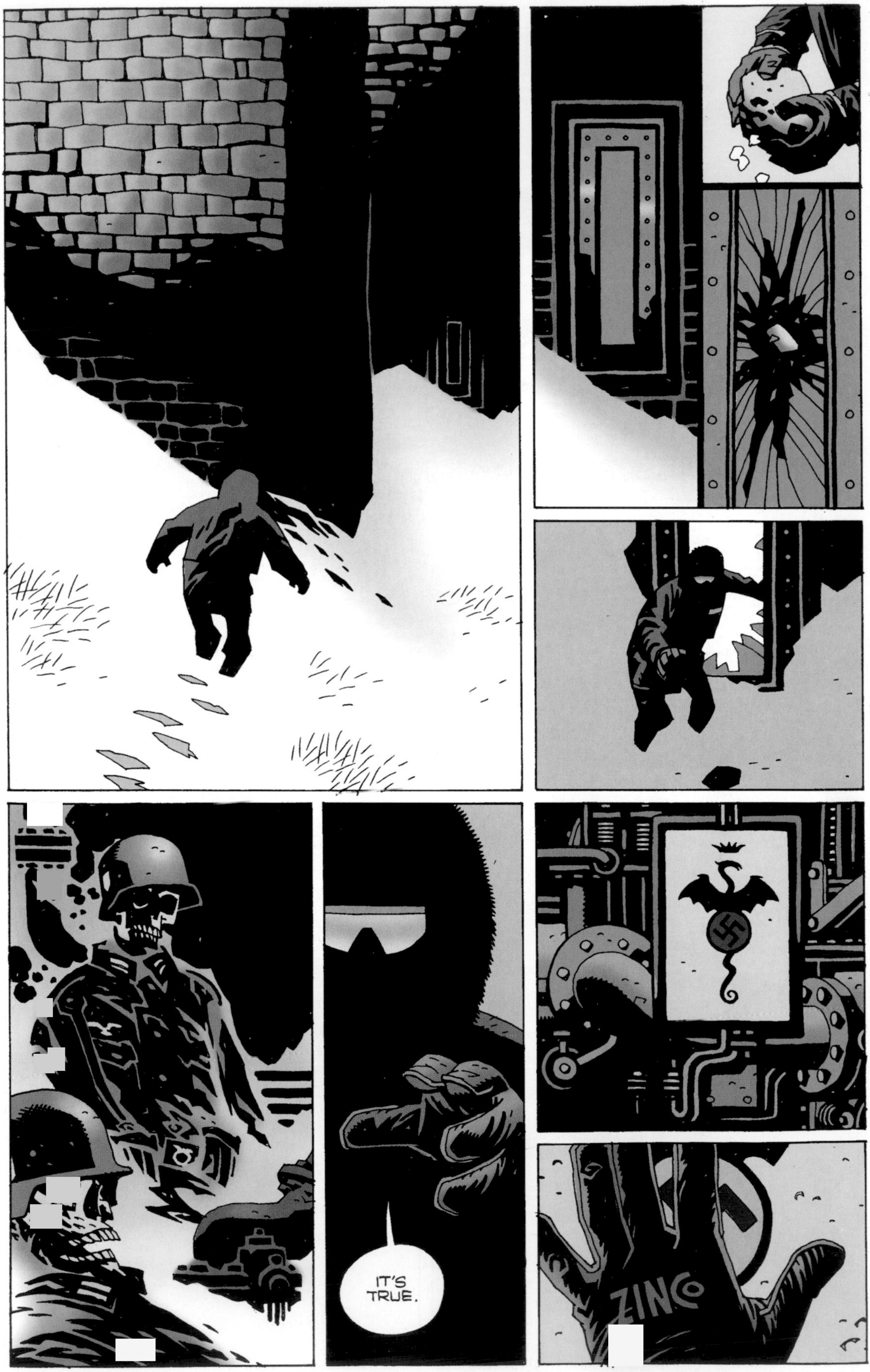
IT'S TRUE.
ZINC

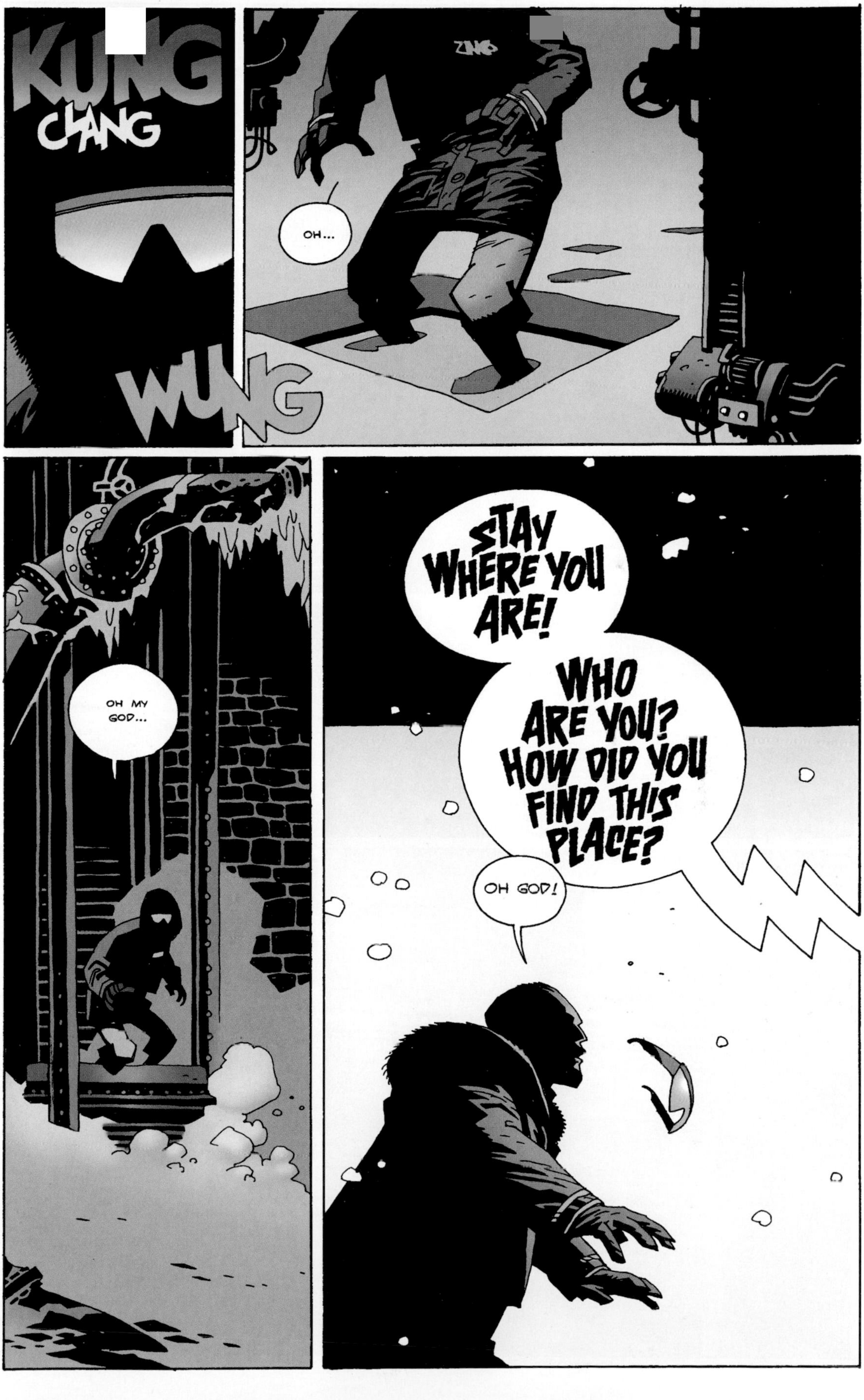
KUNG
CLANG
WUNG
ZING
OH...
OH MY GOD...
STAY WHERE YOU ARE!
WHO ARE YOU? HOW DID YOU FIND THIS PLACE?
OH GOD!

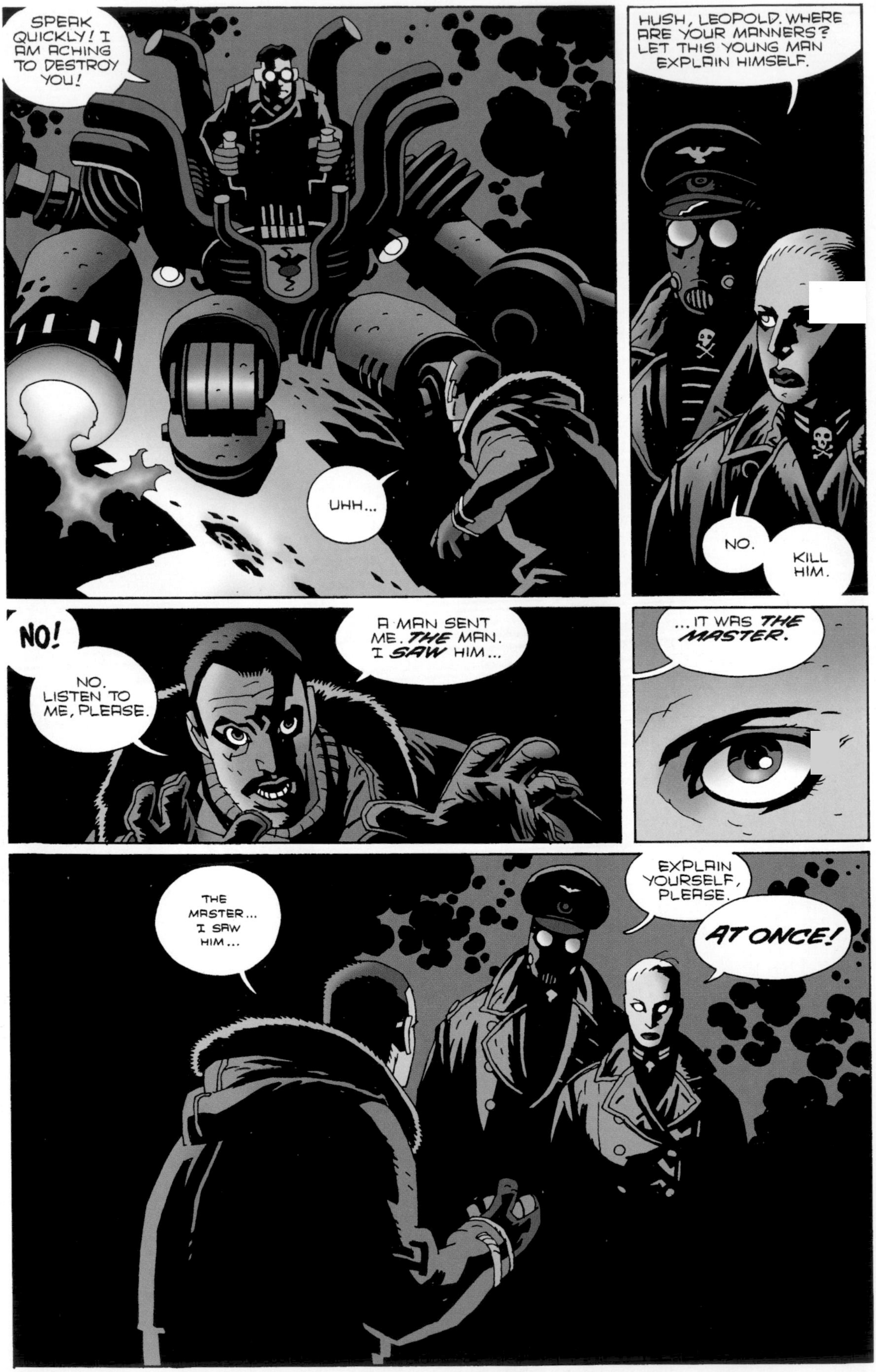
SPEAK QUICKLY! I AM ACHING TO DESTROY YOU!
UHH...
HUSH, LEOPOLD. WHERE ARE YOUR MANNERS? LET THIS YOUNG MAN EXPLAIN HIMSELF.
NO.
KILL HIM.
NO!
NO. LISTEN TO ME, PLEASE.
A MAN SENT ME. THE MAN. I SAW HIM...
...IT WAS THE MASTER.
THE MASTER... I SAW HIM...
EXPLAIN YOURSELF, PLEASE.
AT ONCE!

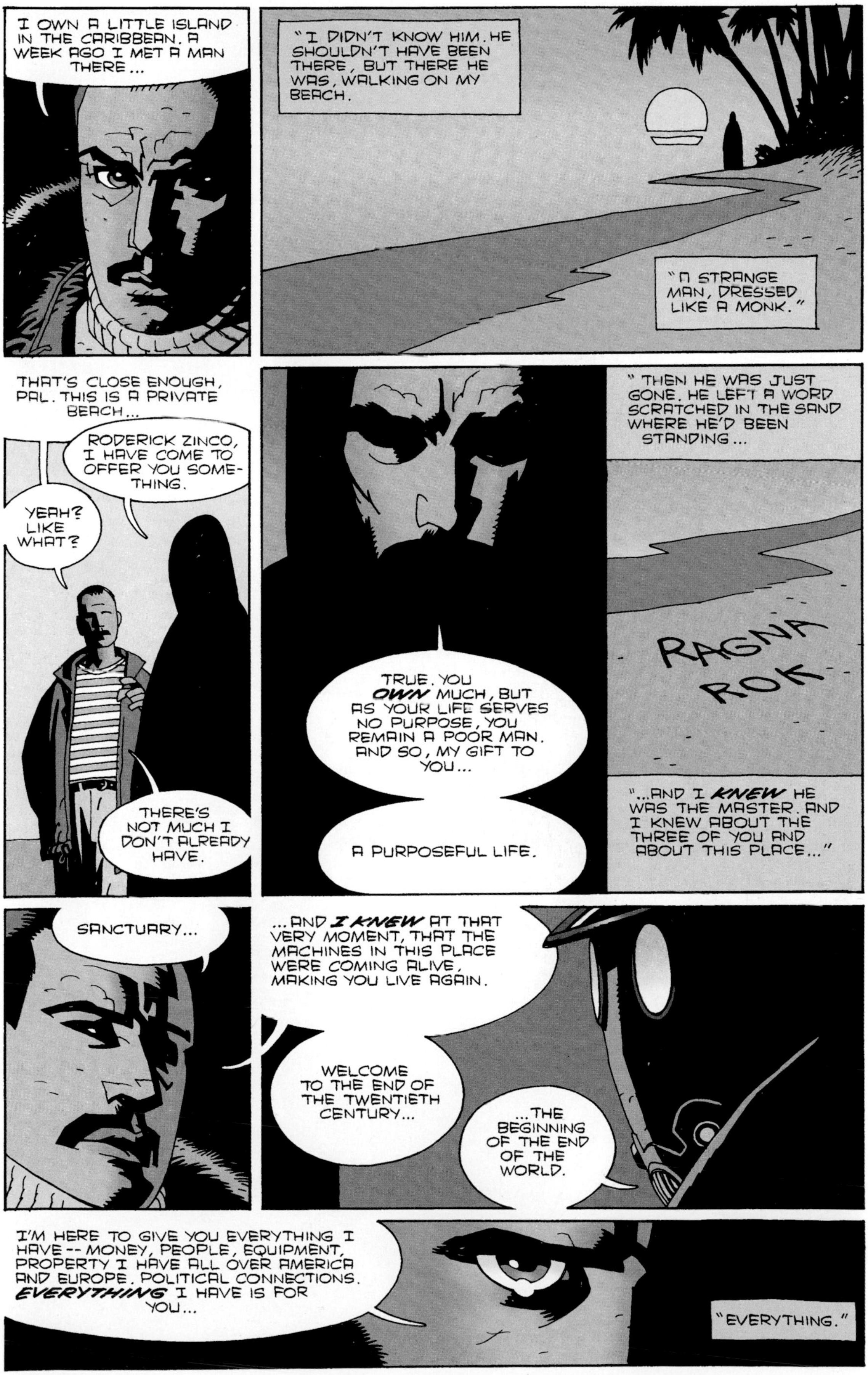
I OWN A LITTLE ISLAND IN THE CARIBBEAN. A WEEK AGO I MET A MAN THERE...
"I DIDN'T KNOW HIM. HE SHOULDN'T HAVE BEEN THERE, BUT THERE HE WAS, WALKING ON MY BEACH.
"A STRANGE MAN, DRESSED LIKE A MONK."
THAT'S CLOSE ENOUGH, PAL. THIS IS A PRIVATE BEACH...
RODERICK ZINCO, I HAVE COME TO OFFER YOU SOMETHING.
YEAH? LIKE WHAT?
THERE'S NOT MUCH I DON'T ALREADY HAVE.
TRUE. YOU OWN MUCH, BUT AS YOUR LIFE SERVES NO PURPOSE, YOU REMAIN A POOR MAN. AND SO, MY GIFT TO YOU...
A PURPOSEFUL LIFE.
" THEN HE WAS JUST GONE. HE LEFT A WORD SCRATCHED IN THE SAND WHERE HE'D BEEN STANDING...
RAGNA ROK
"...AND I KNEW HE WAS THE MASTER. AND I KNEW ABOUT THE THREE OF YOU AND ABOUT THIS PLACE..."
SANCTUARY...
...AND I KNEW AT THAT VERY MOMENT, THAT THE MACHINES IN THIS PLACE WERE COMING ALIVE, MAKING YOU LIVE AGAIN.
WELCOME TO THE END OF THE TWENTIETH CENTURY...
...THE BEGINNING OF THE END OF THE WORLD.
I'M HERE TO GIVE YOU EVERYTHING I HAVE -- MONEY, PEOPLE, EQUIPMENT, PROPERTY I HAVE ALL OVER AMERICA AND EUROPE. POLITICAL CONNECTIONS. EVERYTHING I HAVE IS FOR YOU...
"EVERYTHING."

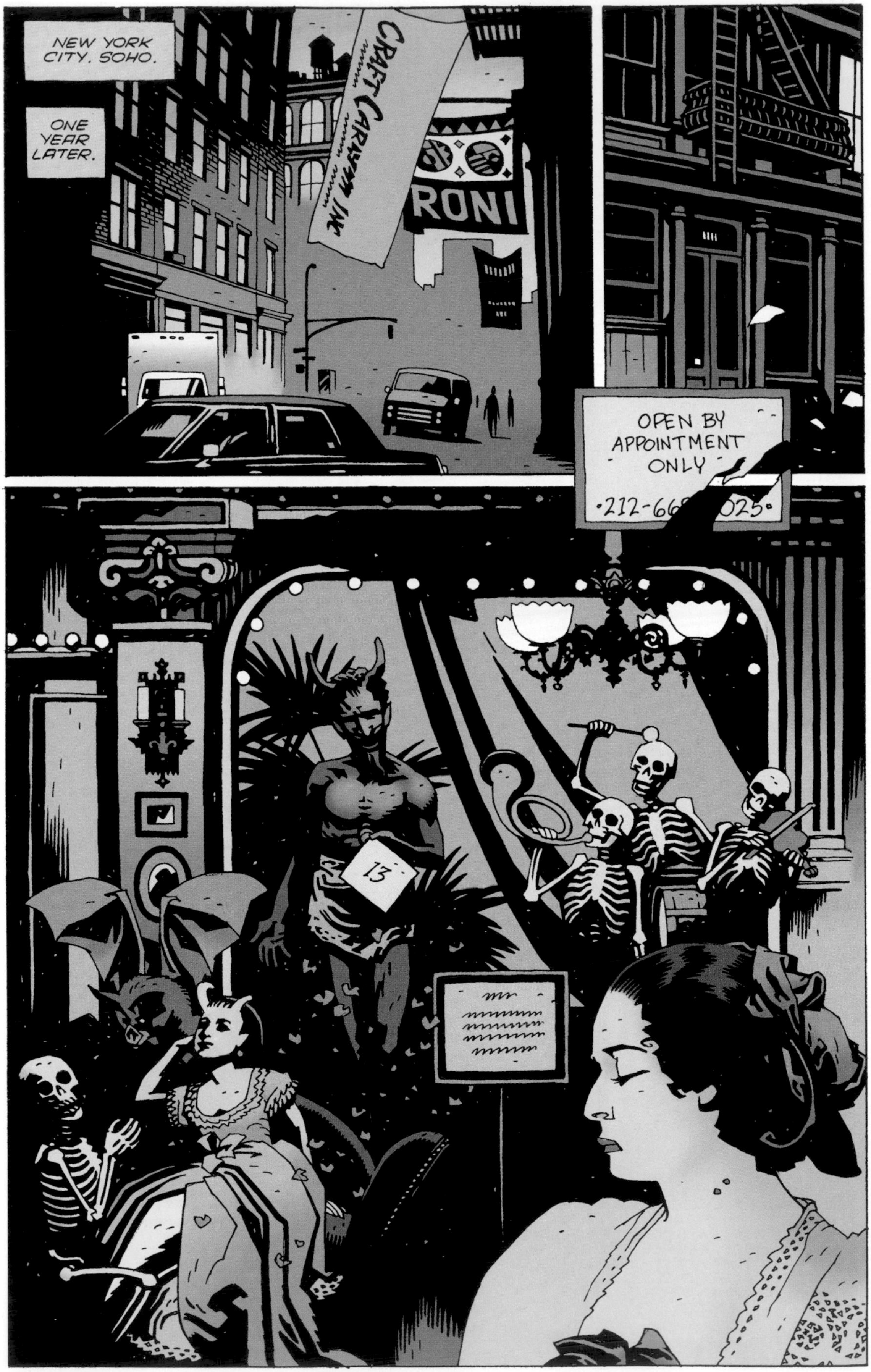
NEW YORK CITY. SOHO.
ONE YEAR LATER.
CRAFT CARAVAN INC
RONI
OPEN BY APPOINTMENT ONLY
13

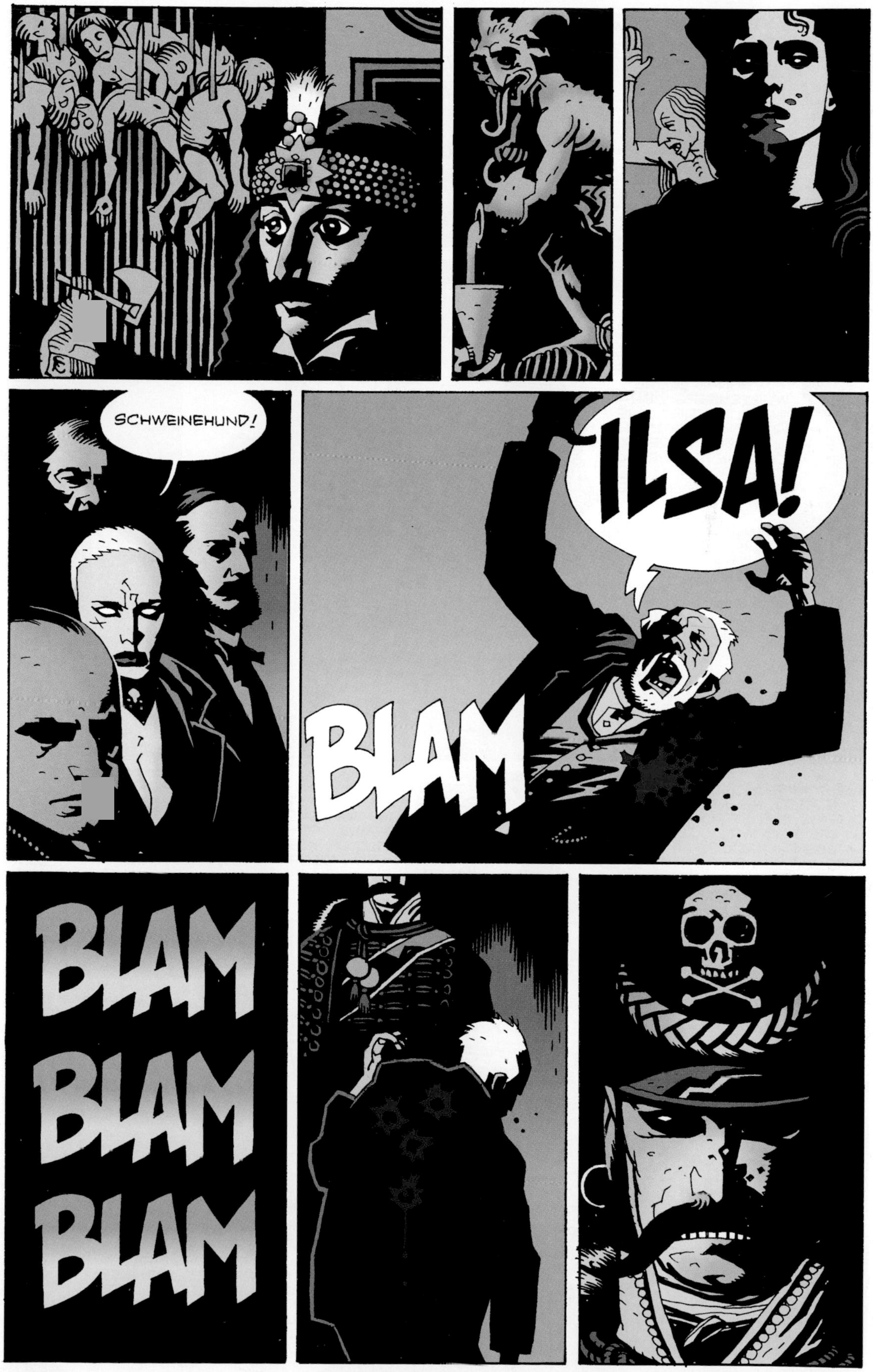
SCHWEINEHUND!
ILSA!
BLAM
BLAM
BLAM
BLAM

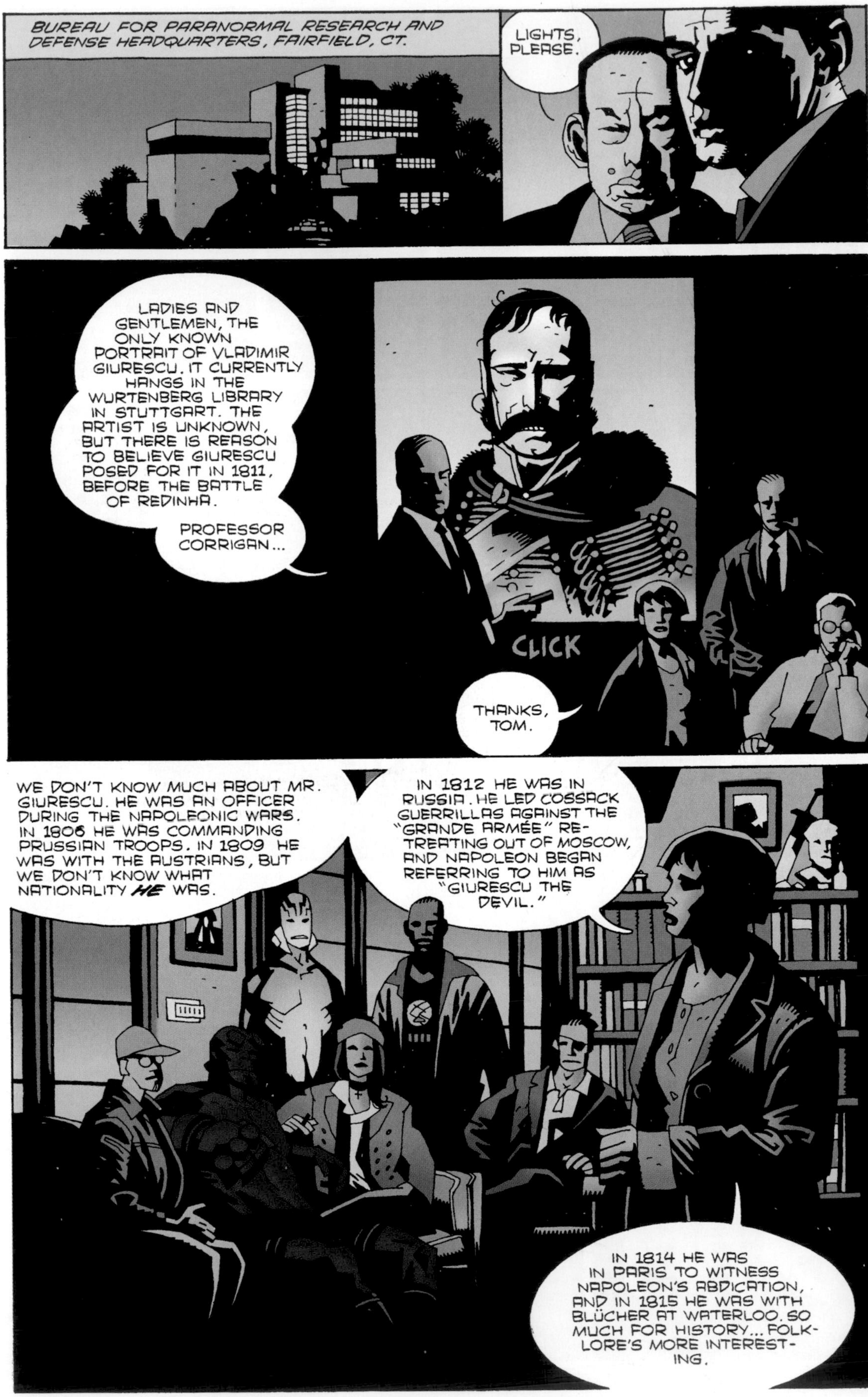
BUREAU FOR PARANORMAL RESEARCH AND DEFENSE HEADQUARTERS, FAIRFIELD, CT.
LIGHTS, PLEASE.
LADIES AND GENTLEMEN, THE ONLY KNOWN PORTRAIT OF VLADIMIR GIURESCU. IT CURRENTLY HANGS IN THE WURTENBERG LIBRARY IN STUTTGART. THE ARTIST IS UNKNOWN, BUT THERE IS REASON TO BELIEVE GIURESCU POSED FOR IT IN 1811, BEFORE THE BATTLE OF REDINHA.
PROFESSOR CORRIGAN...
CLICK
THANKS, TOM.
WE DON'T KNOW MUCH ABOUT MR. GIURESCU. HE WAS AN OFFICER DURING THE NAPOLEONIC WARS. IN 1806 HE WAS COMMANDING PRUSSIAN TROOPS. IN 1809 HE WAS WITH THE AUSTRIANS, BUT WE DON'T KNOW WHAT NATIONALITY *HE* WAS.
IN 1812 HE WAS IN RUSSIA. HE LED COSSACK GUERRILLAS AGAINST THE "GRANDE ARMÉE" RETREATING OUT OF MOSCOW, AND NAPOLEON BEGAN REFERRING TO HIM AS "GIURESCU THE DEVIL."
IN 1814 HE WAS IN PARIS TO WITNESS NAPOLEON'S ABDICATION, AND IN 1815 HE WAS WITH BLÜCHER AT WATERLOO. SO MUCH FOR HISTORY... FOLKLORE'S MORE INTERESTING.

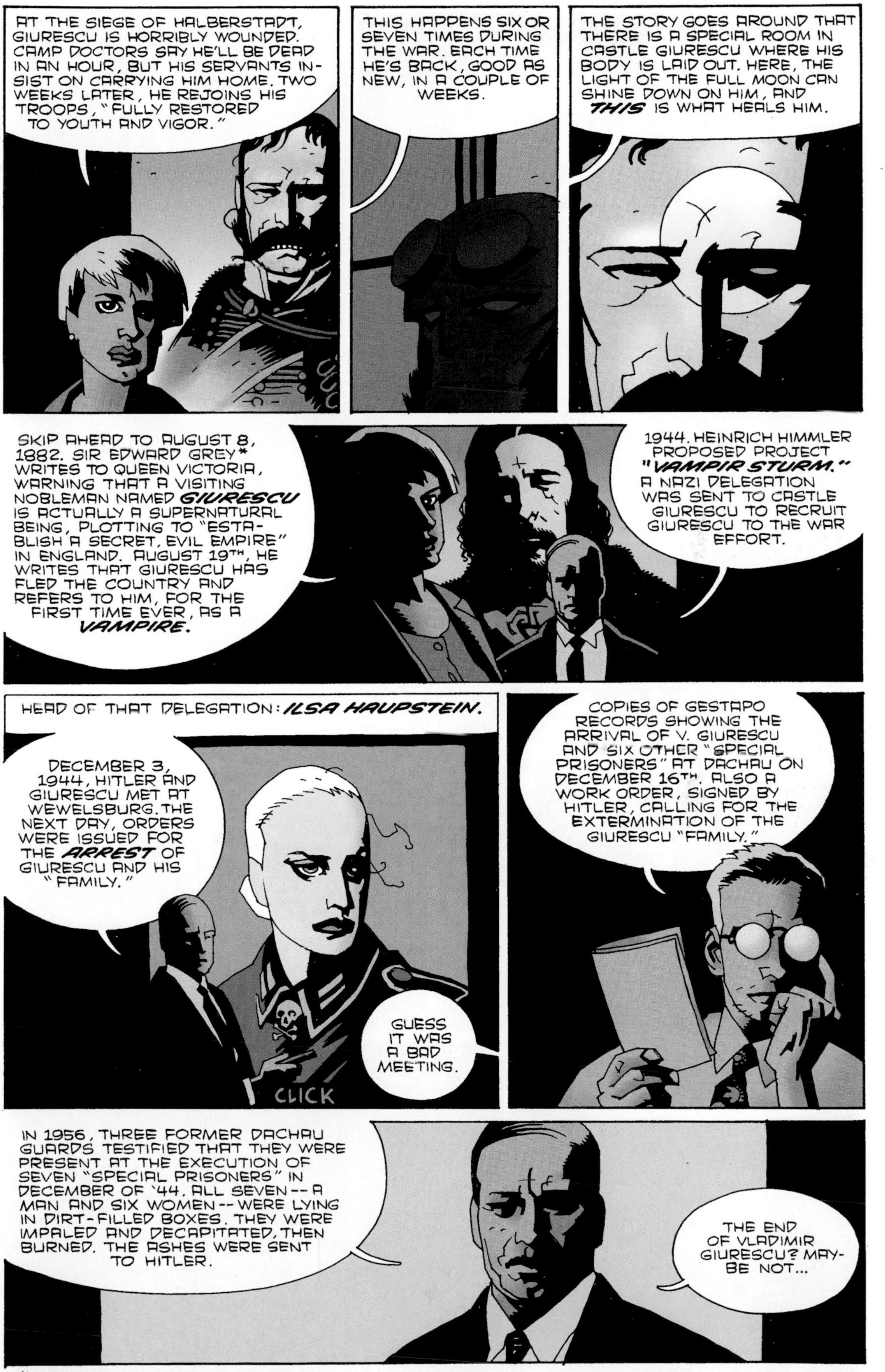
AT THE SIEGE OF HALBERSTADT, GIURESCU IS HORRIBLY WOUNDED. CAMP DOCTORS SAY HE'LL BE DEAD IN AN HOUR, BUT HIS SERVANTS INSIST ON CARRYING HIM HOME. TWO WEEKS LATER, HE REJOINS HIS TROOPS, "FULLY RESTORED TO YOUTH AND VIGOR."
THIS HAPPENS SIX OR SEVEN TIMES DURING THE WAR. EACH TIME HE'S BACK, GOOD AS NEW, IN A COUPLE OF WEEKS.
THE STORY GOES AROUND THAT THERE IS A SPECIAL ROOM IN CASTLE GIURESCU WHERE HIS BODY IS LAID OUT. HERE, THE LIGHT OF THE FULL MOON CAN SHINE DOWN ON HIM, AND THIS IS WHAT HEALS HIM.
SKIP AHEAD TO AUGUST 8, 1882. SIR EDWARD GREY* WRITES TO QUEEN VICTORIA, WARNING THAT A VISITING NOBLEMAN NAMED GIURESCU IS ACTUALLY A SUPERNATURAL BEING, PLOTTING TO "ESTABLISH A SECRET, EVIL EMPIRE" IN ENGLAND. AUGUST 19TH, HE WRITES THAT GIURESCU HAS FLED THE COUNTRY AND REFERS TO HIM, FOR THE FIRST TIME EVER, AS A VAMPIRE.
1944. HEINRICH HIMMLER PROPOSED PROJECT "VAMPIR STURM." A NAZI DELEGATION WAS SENT TO CASTLE GIURESCU TO RECRUIT GIURESCU TO THE WAR EFFORT.
HEAD OF THAT DELEGATION: ILSA HAUPSTEIN.
DECEMBER 3, 1944, HITLER AND GIURESCU MET AT WEWELSBURG. THE NEXT DAY, ORDERS WERE ISSUED FOR THE ARREST OF GIURESCU AND HIS "FAMILY."
GUESS IT WAS A BAD MEETING.
CLICK
COPIES OF GESTAPO RECORDS SHOWING THE ARRIVAL OF V. GIURESCU AND SIX OTHER "SPECIAL PRISONERS" AT DACHAU ON DECEMBER 16TH. ALSO A WORK ORDER, SIGNED BY HITLER, CALLING FOR THE EXTERMINATION OF THE GIURESCU "FAMILY."
IN 1956, THREE FORMER DACHAU GUARDS TESTIFIED THAT THEY WERE PRESENT AT THE EXECUTION OF SEVEN "SPECIAL PRISONERS" IN DECEMBER OF '44. ALL SEVEN -- A MAN AND SIX WOMEN -- WERE LYING IN DIRT-FILLED BOXES. THEY WERE IMPALED AND DECAPITATED, THEN BURNED. THE ASHES WERE SENT TO HITLER.
THE END OF VLADIMIR GIURESCU? MAYBE NOT...

***** *FAMOUS NINETEENTH-CENTURY PARANORMAL INVESTIGATOR*

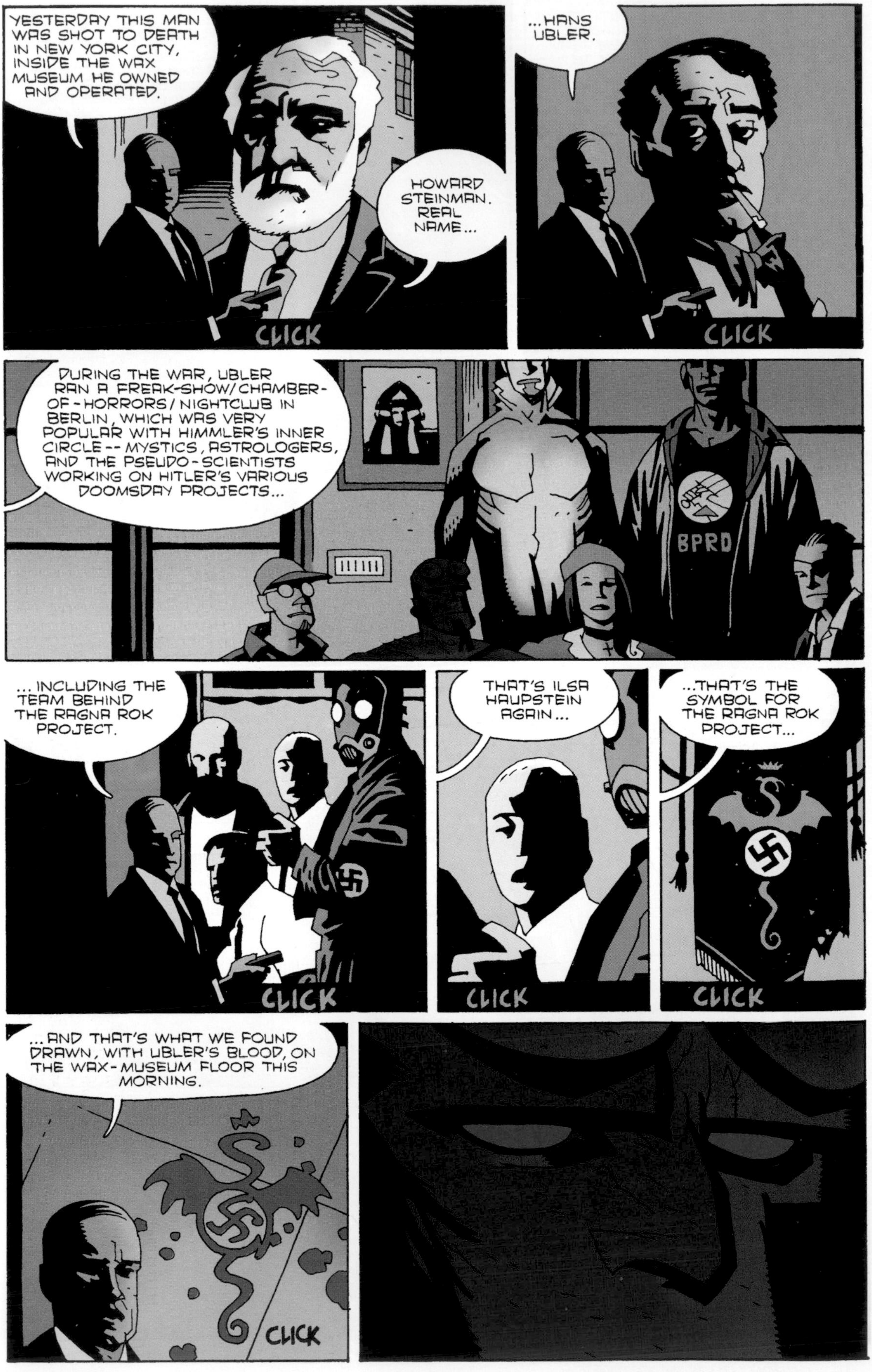
YESTERDAY THIS MAN WAS SHOT TO DEATH IN NEW YORK CITY, INSIDE THE WAX MUSEUM HE OWNED AND OPERATED.
HOWARD STEINMAN. REAL NAME...
CLICK
...HANS UBLER.
CLICK
DURING THE WAR, UBLER RAN A FREAK-SHOW/CHAMBER-OF-HORRORS/NIGHTCLUB IN BERLIN, WHICH WAS VERY POPULAR WITH HIMMLER'S INNER CIRCLE -- MYSTICS, ASTROLOGERS, AND THE PSEUDO-SCIENTISTS WORKING ON HITLER'S VARIOUS DOOMSDAY PROJECTS...
BPRD
...INCLUDING THE TEAM BEHIND THE RAGNA ROK PROJECT.
CLICK
THAT'S ILSA HAUPSTEIN AGAIN...
CLICK
...THAT'S THE SYMBOL FOR THE RAGNA ROK PROJECT...
CLICK
...AND THAT'S WHAT WE FOUND DRAWN, WITH UBLER'S BLOOD, ON THE WAX-MUSEUM FLOOR THIS MORNING.
CLICK

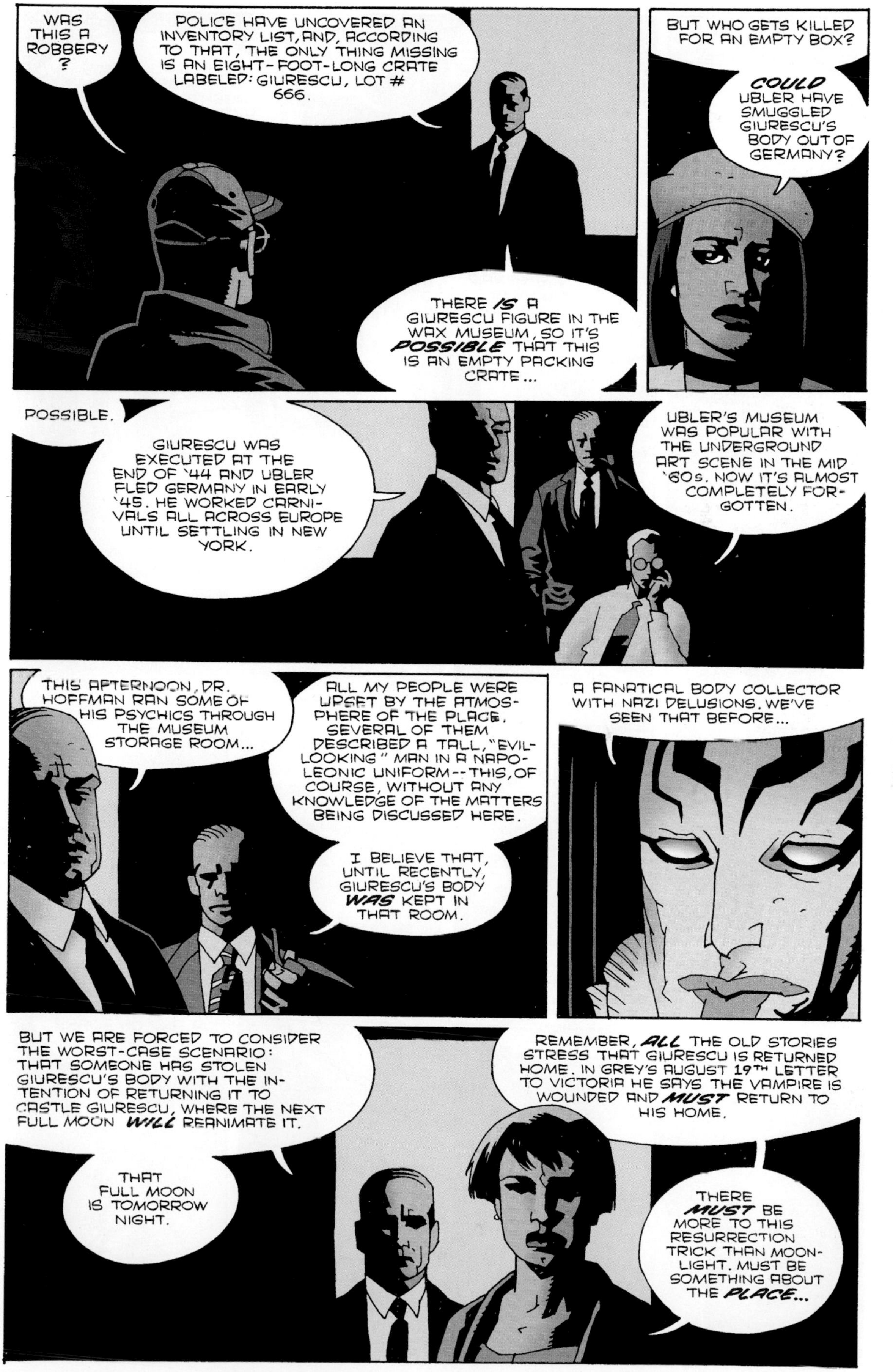
WAS THIS A ROBBERY ?
POLICE HAVE UNCOVERED AN INVENTORY LIST, AND, ACCORDING TO THAT, THE ONLY THING MISSING IS AN EIGHT-FOOT-LONG CRATE LABELED: GIURESCU, LOT # 666.
THERE IS A GIURESCU FIGURE IN THE WAX MUSEUM, SO IT'S POSSIBLE THAT THIS IS AN EMPTY PACKING CRATE...
BUT WHO GETS KILLED FOR AN EMPTY BOX?
COULD UBLER HAVE SMUGGLED GIURESCU'S BODY OUT OF GERMANY?
POSSIBLE.
GIURESCU WAS EXECUTED AT THE END OF '44 AND UBLER FLED GERMANY IN EARLY '45. HE WORKED CARNIVALS ALL ACROSS EUROPE UNTIL SETTLING IN NEW YORK.
UBLER'S MUSEUM WAS POPULAR WITH THE UNDERGROUND ART SCENE IN THE MID '60s. NOW IT'S ALMOST COMPLETELY FORGOTTEN.
THIS AFTERNOON, DR. HOFFMAN RAN SOME OF HIS PSYCHICS THROUGH THE MUSEUM STORAGE ROOM...
ALL MY PEOPLE WERE UPSET BY THE ATMOSPHERE OF THE PLACE. SEVERAL OF THEM DESCRIBED A TALL, "EVIL-LOOKING" MAN IN A NAPOLEONIC UNIFORM -- THIS, OF COURSE, WITHOUT ANY KNOWLEDGE OF THE MATTERS BEING DISCUSSED HERE.
I BELIEVE THAT, UNTIL RECENTLY, GIURESCU'S BODY WAS KEPT IN THAT ROOM.
A FANATICAL BODY COLLECTOR WITH NAZI DELUSIONS. WE'VE SEEN THAT BEFORE...
BUT WE ARE FORCED TO CONSIDER THE WORST-CASE SCENARIO: THAT SOMEONE HAS STOLEN GIURESCU'S BODY WITH THE INTENTION OF RETURNING IT TO CASTLE GIURESCU, WHERE THE NEXT FULL MOON WILL REANIMATE IT.
THAT FULL MOON IS TOMORROW NIGHT.
REMEMBER, ALL THE OLD STORIES STRESS THAT GIURESCU IS RETURNED HOME. IN GREY'S AUGUST 19TH LETTER TO VICTORIA HE SAYS THE VAMPIRE IS WOUNDED AND MUST RETURN TO HIS HOME.
THERE MUST BE MORE TO THIS RESURRECTION TRICK THAN MOONLIGHT. MUST BE SOMETHING ABOUT THE PLACE...

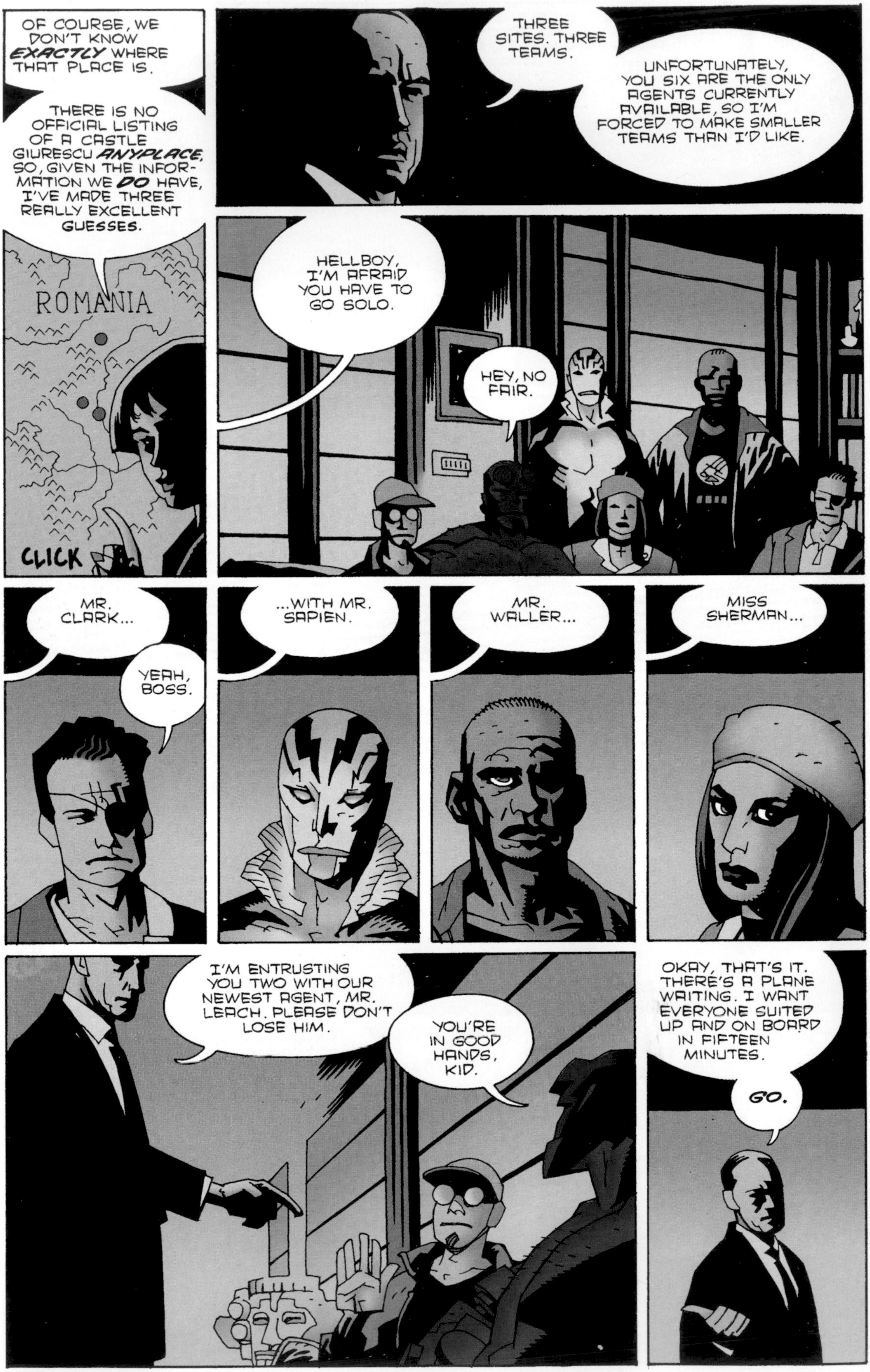
OF COURSE, WE DON'T KNOW EXACTLY WHERE THAT PLACE IS.
THERE IS NO OFFICIAL LISTING OF A CASTLE GIURESCU ANYPLACE. SO, GIVEN THE INFORMATION WE DO HAVE, I'VE MADE THREE REALLY EXCELLENT GUESSES.
ROMANIA
CLICK
THREE SITES. THREE TEAMS.
UNFORTUNATELY, YOU SIX ARE THE ONLY AGENTS CURRENTLY AVAILABLE, SO I'M FORCED TO MAKE SMALLER TEAMS THAN I'D LIKE.
HELLBOY, I'M AFRAID YOU HAVE TO GO SOLO.
HEY, NO FAIR.
MR. CLARK...
YEAH, BOSS.
...WITH MR. SAPIEN.
MR. WALLER...
MISS SHERMAN...
I'M ENTRUSTING YOU TWO WITH OUR NEWEST AGENT, MR. LEACH. PLEASE DON'T LOSE HIM.
YOU'RE IN GOOD HANDS, KID.
OKAY, THAT'S IT. THERE'S A PLANE WAITING. I WANT EVERYONE SUITED UP AND ON BOARD IN FIFTEEN MINUTES.
GO.

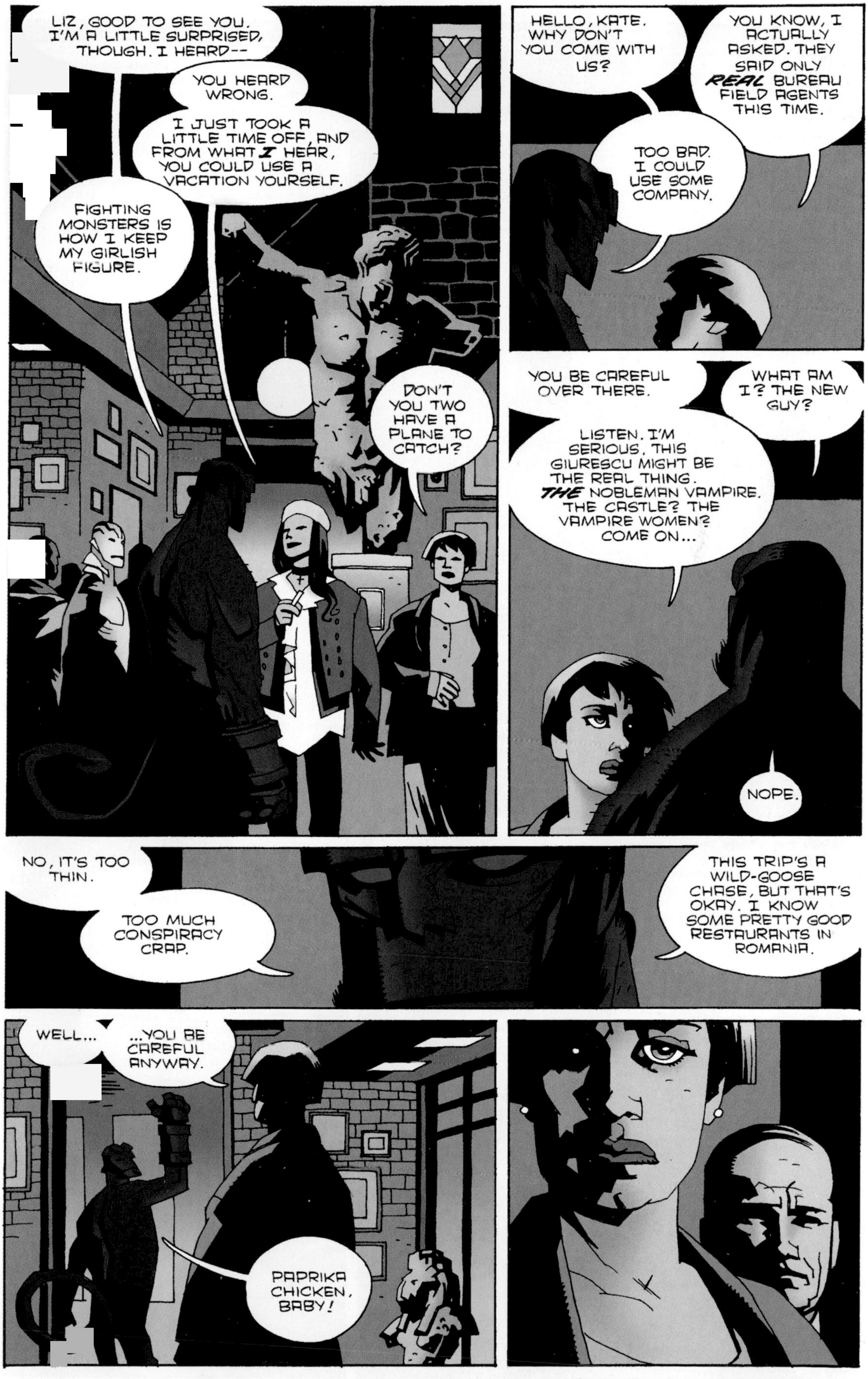
LIZ, GOOD TO SEE YOU. I'M A LITTLE SURPRISED, THOUGH. I HEARD--
YOU HEARD WRONG.
I JUST TOOK A LITTLE TIME OFF, AND FROM WHAT I HEAR, YOU COULD USE A VACATION YOURSELF.
FIGHTING MONSTERS IS HOW I KEEP MY GIRLISH FIGURE.
DON'T YOU TWO HAVE A PLANE TO CATCH?
HELLO, KATE. WHY DON'T YOU COME WITH US?
YOU KNOW, I ACTUALLY ASKED. THEY SAID ONLY REAL BUREAU FIELD AGENTS THIS TIME.
TOO BAD. I COULD USE SOME COMPANY.
YOU BE CAREFUL OVER THERE.
WHAT AM I? THE NEW GUY?
LISTEN. I'M SERIOUS. THIS GIURESCU MIGHT BE THE REAL THING. THE NOBLEMAN VAMPIRE. THE CASTLE? THE VAMPIRE WOMEN? COME ON...
NOPE.
NO, IT'S TOO THIN.
TOO MUCH CONSPIRACY CRAP.
THIS TRIP'S A WILD-GOOSE CHASE, BUT THAT'S OKAY. I KNOW SOME PRETTY GOOD RESTAURANTS IN ROMANIA.
WELL...
...YOU BE CAREFUL ANYWAY.
PAPRIKA CHICKEN, BABY!

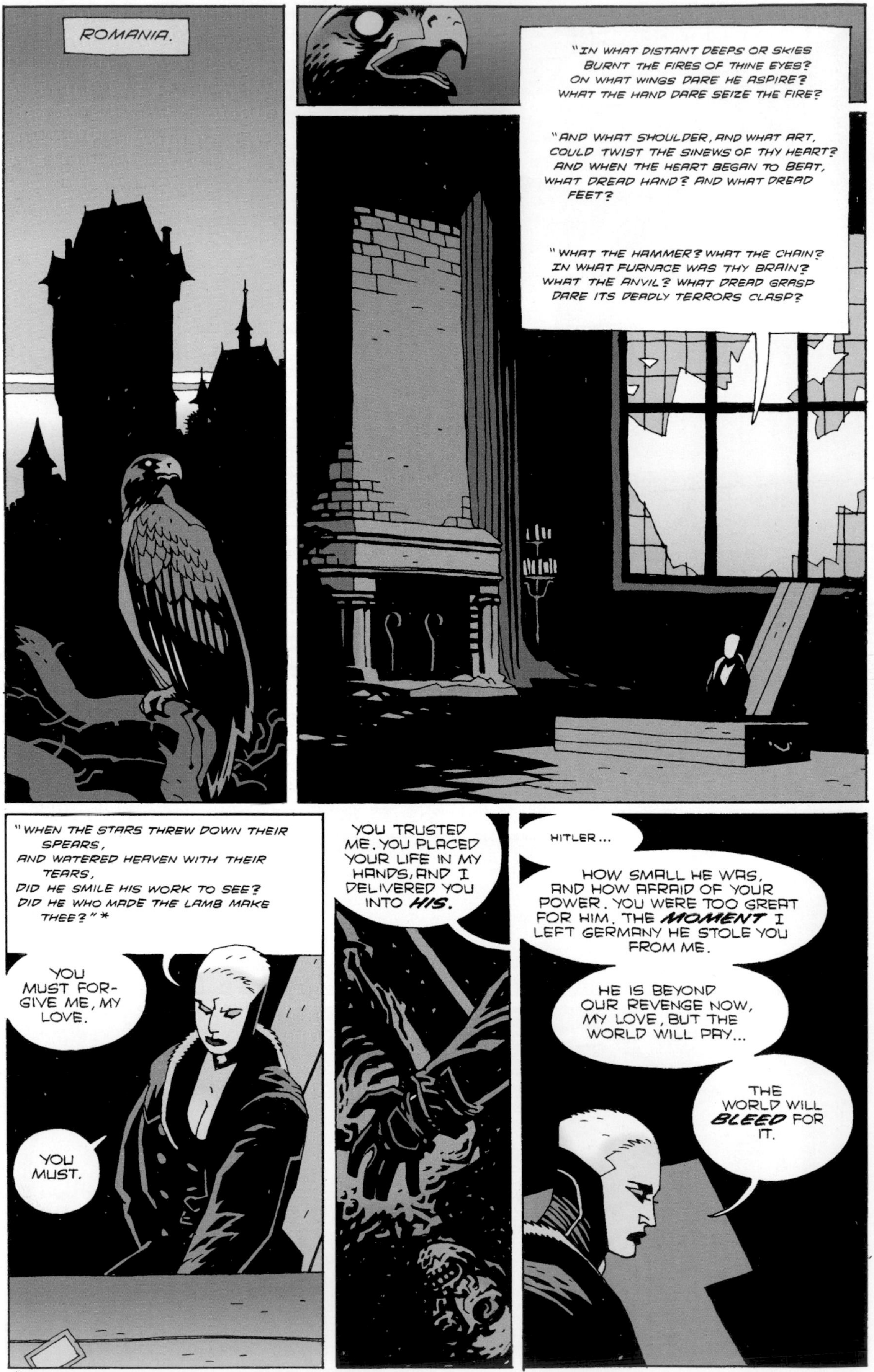
ROMANIA.
"IN WHAT DISTANT DEEPS OR SKIES BURNT THE FIRES OF THINE EYES? ON WHAT WINGS DARE HE ASPIRE? WHAT THE HAND DARE SEIZE THE FIRE?
"AND WHAT SHOULDER, AND WHAT ART, COULD TWIST THE SINEWS OF THY HEART? AND WHEN THE HEART BEGAN TO BEAT, WHAT DREAD HAND? AND WHAT DREAD FEET?
"WHAT THE HAMMER? WHAT THE CHAIN? IN WHAT FURNACE WAS THY BRAIN? WHAT THE ANVIL? WHAT DREAD GRASP DARE ITS DEADLY TERRORS CLASP?
"WHEN THE STARS THREW DOWN THEIR SPEARS, AND WATERED HEAVEN WITH THEIR TEARS, DID HE SMILE HIS WORK TO SEE? DID HE WHO MADE THE LAMB MAKE THEE?" *
YOU MUST FOR-GIVE ME, MY LOVE.
YOU MUST.
YOU TRUSTED ME. YOU PLACED YOUR LIFE IN MY HANDS, AND I DELIVERED YOU INTO HIS.
HITLER...
HOW SMALL HE WAS, AND HOW AFRAID OF YOUR POWER. YOU WERE TOO GREAT FOR HIM. THE MOMENT I LEFT GERMANY HE STOLE YOU FROM ME.
HE IS BEYOND OUR REVENGE NOW, MY LOVE, BUT THE WORLD WILL PAY...
THE WORLD WILL BLEED FOR IT.

* FROM "THE TYGER" BY WILLIAM BLAKE

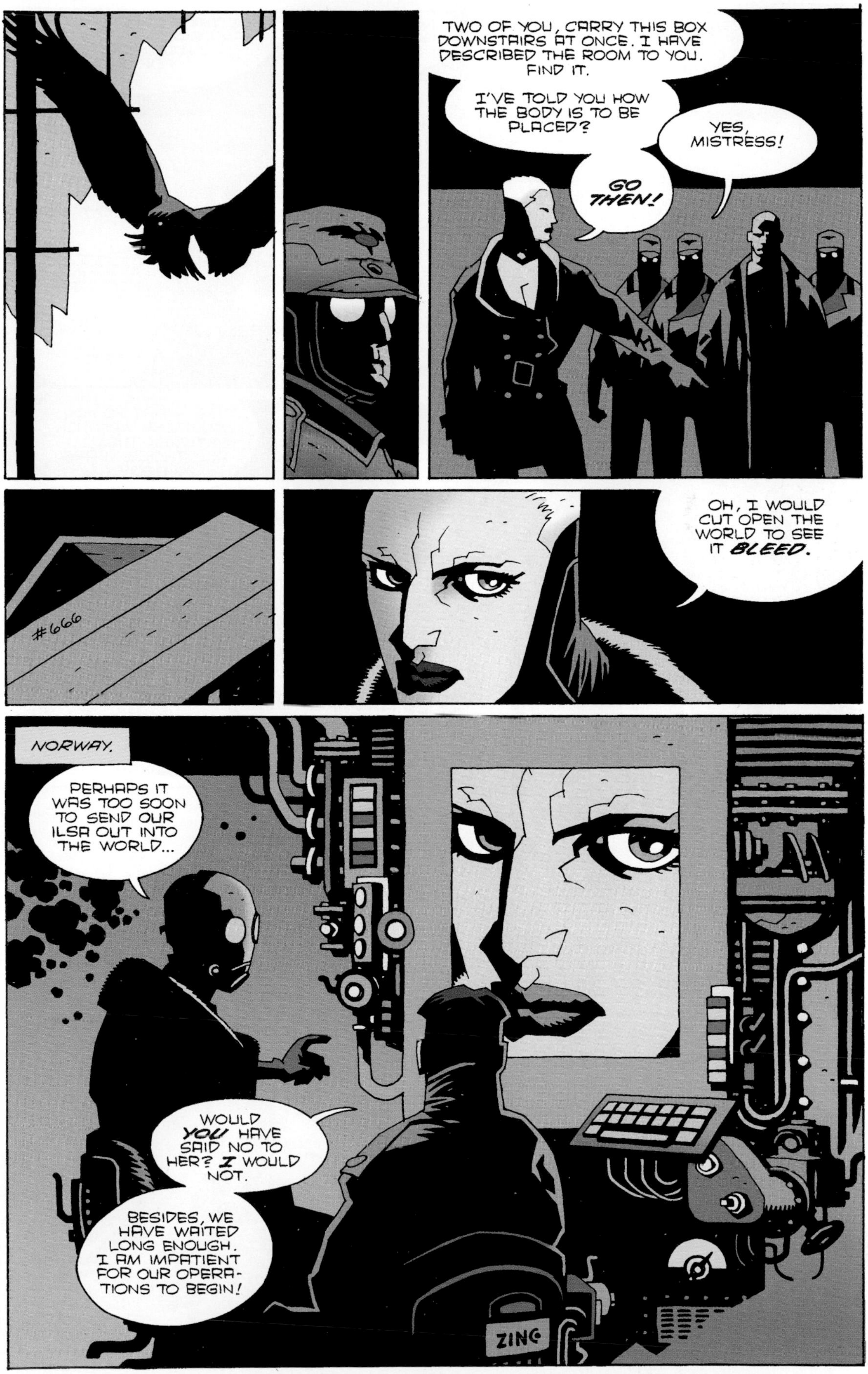
TWO OF YOU, CARRY THIS BOX DOWNSTAIRS AT ONCE. I HAVE DESCRIBED THE ROOM TO YOU. FIND IT.
I'VE TOLD YOU HOW THE BODY IS TO BE PLACED?
YES, MISTRESS!
GO THEN!
#666
OH, I WOULD CUT OPEN THE WORLD TO SEE IT BLEED.
NORWAY.
PERHAPS IT WAS TOO SOON TO SEND OUR ILSA OUT INTO THE WORLD...
WOULD YOU HAVE SAID NO TO HER? I WOULD NOT.
BESIDES, WE HAVE WAITED LONG ENOUGH. I AM IMPATIENT FOR OUR OPERATIONS TO BEGIN!
ZING

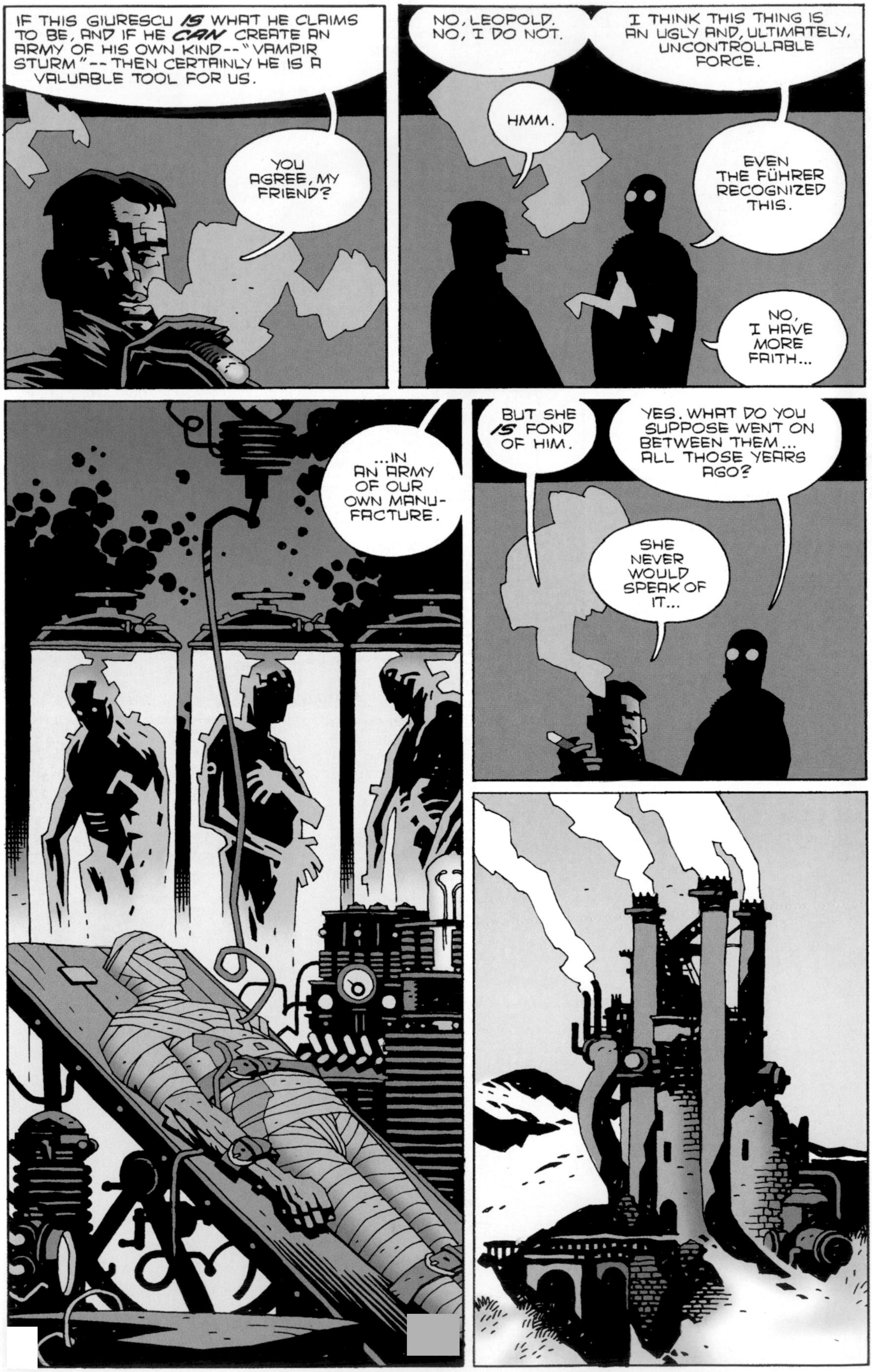
IF THIS GIURESCU IS WHAT HE CLAIMS TO BE, AND IF HE CAN CREATE AN ARMY OF HIS OWN KIND--"VAMPIR STURM"--THEN CERTAINLY HE IS A VALUABLE TOOL FOR US.
YOU AGREE, MY FRIEND?
NO, LEOPOLD. NO, I DO NOT.
I THINK THIS THING IS AN UGLY AND, ULTIMATELY, UNCONTROLLABLE FORCE.
HMM.
EVEN THE FÜHRER RECOGNIZED THIS.
NO, I HAVE MORE FAITH...
...IN AN ARMY OF OUR OWN MANU-FACTURE.
BUT SHE IS FOND OF HIM.
YES. WHAT DO YOU SUPPOSE WENT ON BETWEEN THEM... ALL THOSE YEARS AGO?
SHE NEVER WOULD SPEAK OF IT...

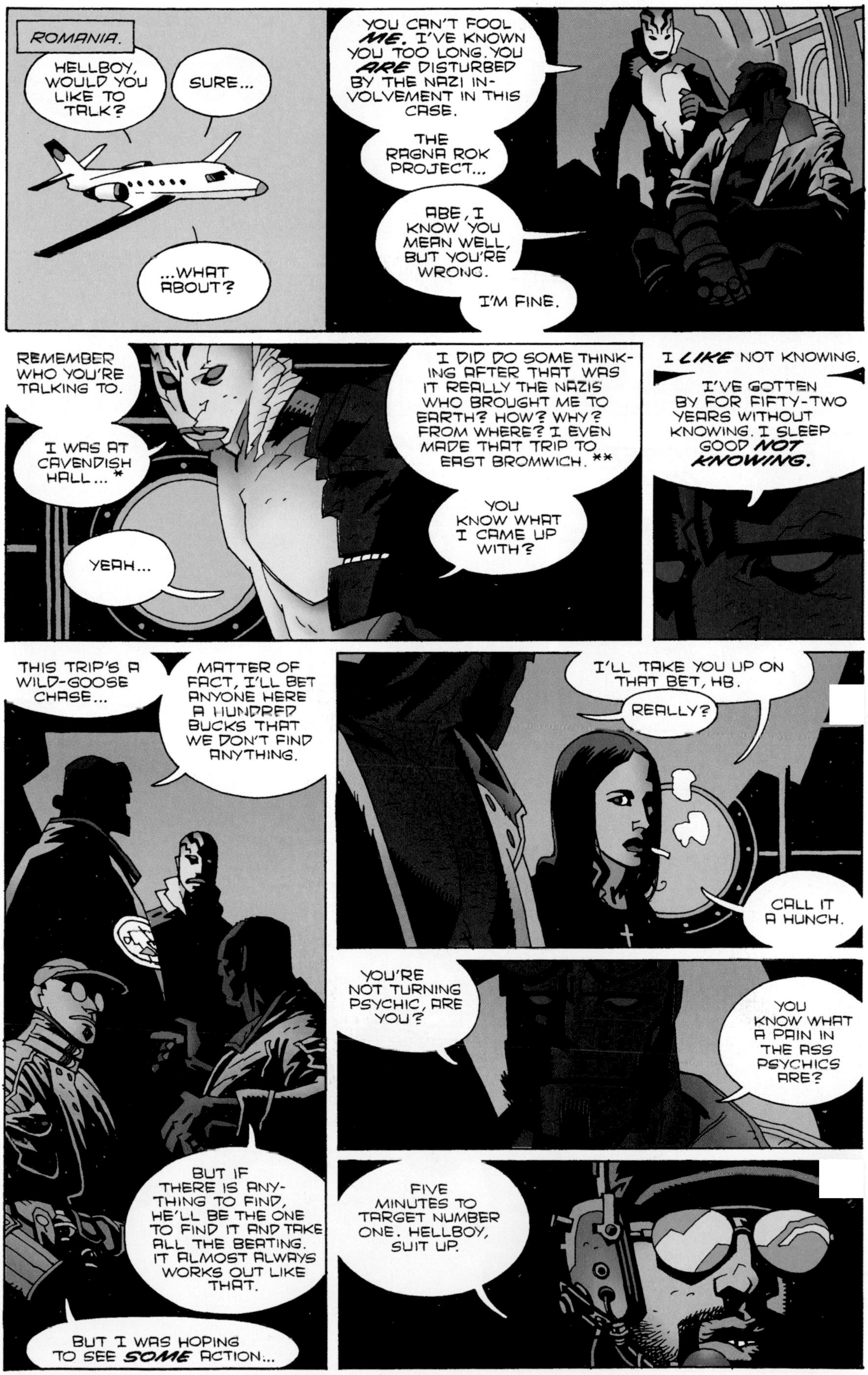
ROMANIA.
HELLBOY, WOULD YOU LIKE TO TALK?
SURE...
...WHAT ABOUT?
YOU CAN'T FOOL ME. I'VE KNOWN YOU TOO LONG. YOU ARE DISTURBED BY THE NAZI INVOLVEMENT IN THIS CASE.
THE RAGNA ROK PROJECT...
ABE, I KNOW YOU MEAN WELL, BUT YOU'RE WRONG.
I'M FINE.
REMEMBER WHO YOU'RE TALKING TO.
I WAS AT CAVENDISH HALL... *
YEAH...
I DID DO SOME THINKING AFTER THAT. WAS IT REALLY THE NAZIS WHO BROUGHT ME TO EARTH? HOW? WHY? FROM WHERE? I EVEN MADE THAT TRIP TO EAST BROMWICH. **
YOU KNOW WHAT I CAME UP WITH?
I LIKE NOT KNOWING.
I'VE GOTTEN BY FOR FIFTY-TWO YEARS WITHOUT KNOWING. I SLEEP GOOD NOT KNOWING.
THIS TRIP'S A WILD-GOOSE CHASE...
MATTER OF FACT, I'LL BET ANYONE HERE A HUNDRED BUCKS THAT WE DON'T FIND ANYTHING.
BUT IF THERE IS ANYTHING TO FIND, HE'LL BE THE ONE TO FIND IT AND TAKE ALL THE BEATING. IT ALMOST ALWAYS WORKS OUT LIKE THAT.
BUT I WAS HOPING TO SEE SOME ACTION...
I'LL TAKE YOU UP ON THAT BET, HB.
REALLY?
CALL IT A HUNCH.
YOU'RE NOT TURNING PSYCHIC, ARE YOU?
YOU KNOW WHAT A PAIN IN THE ASS PSYCHICS ARE?
FIVE MINUTES TO TARGET NUMBER ONE. HELLBOY, SUIT UP.

* HELLBOY: SEED OF DESTRUCTION

** HELLBOY: THE CHAINED COFFIN

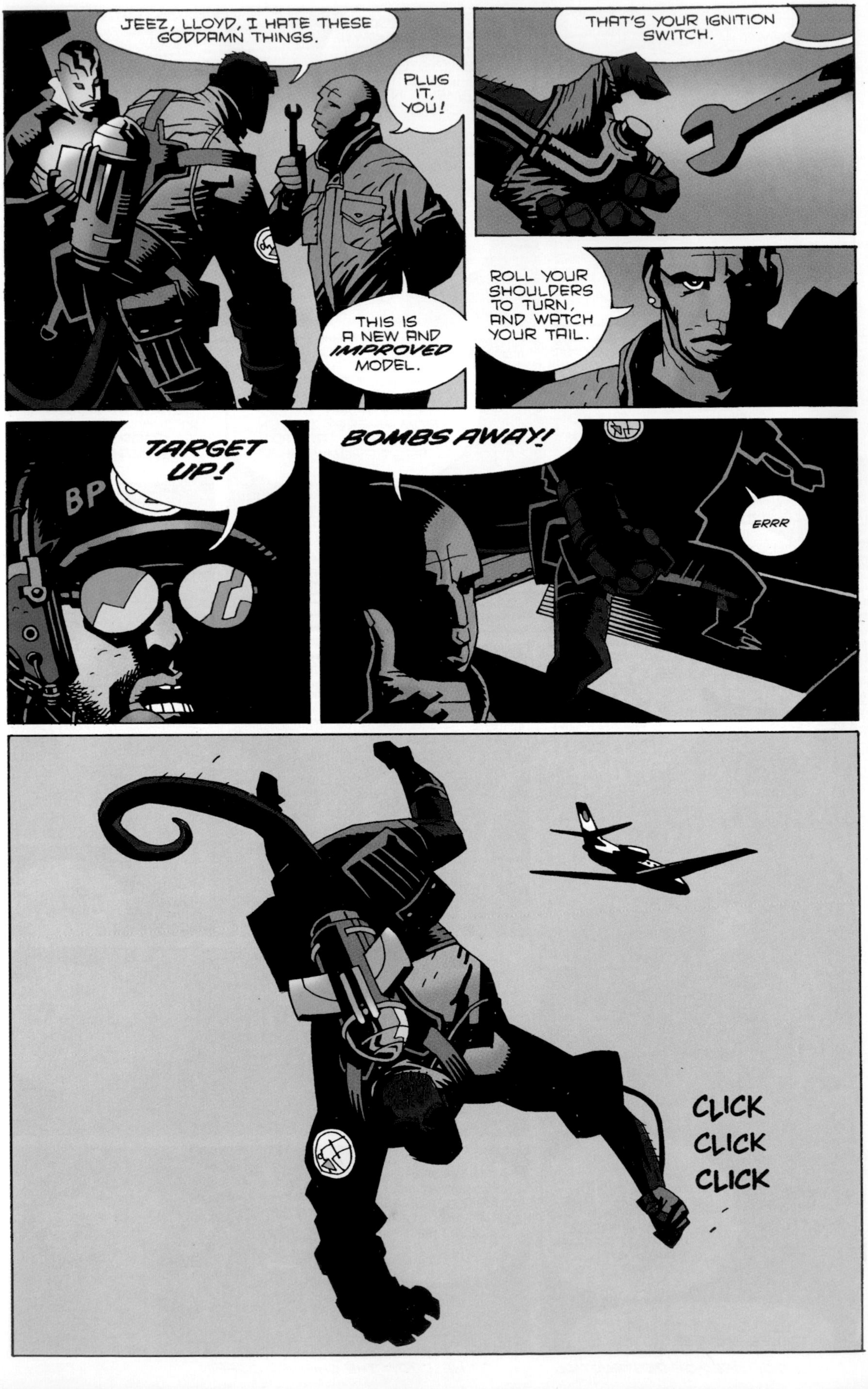
JEEZ, LLOYD, I HATE THESE GODDAMN THINGS.
PLUG IT, YOU!
THIS IS A NEW AND *IMPROVED* MODEL.
THAT'S YOUR IGNITION SWITCH.
ROLL YOUR SHOULDERS TO TURN, AND WATCH YOUR TAIL.
TARGET UP!
BP
BOMBS AWAY!
ERRR
CLICK
CLICK
CLICK

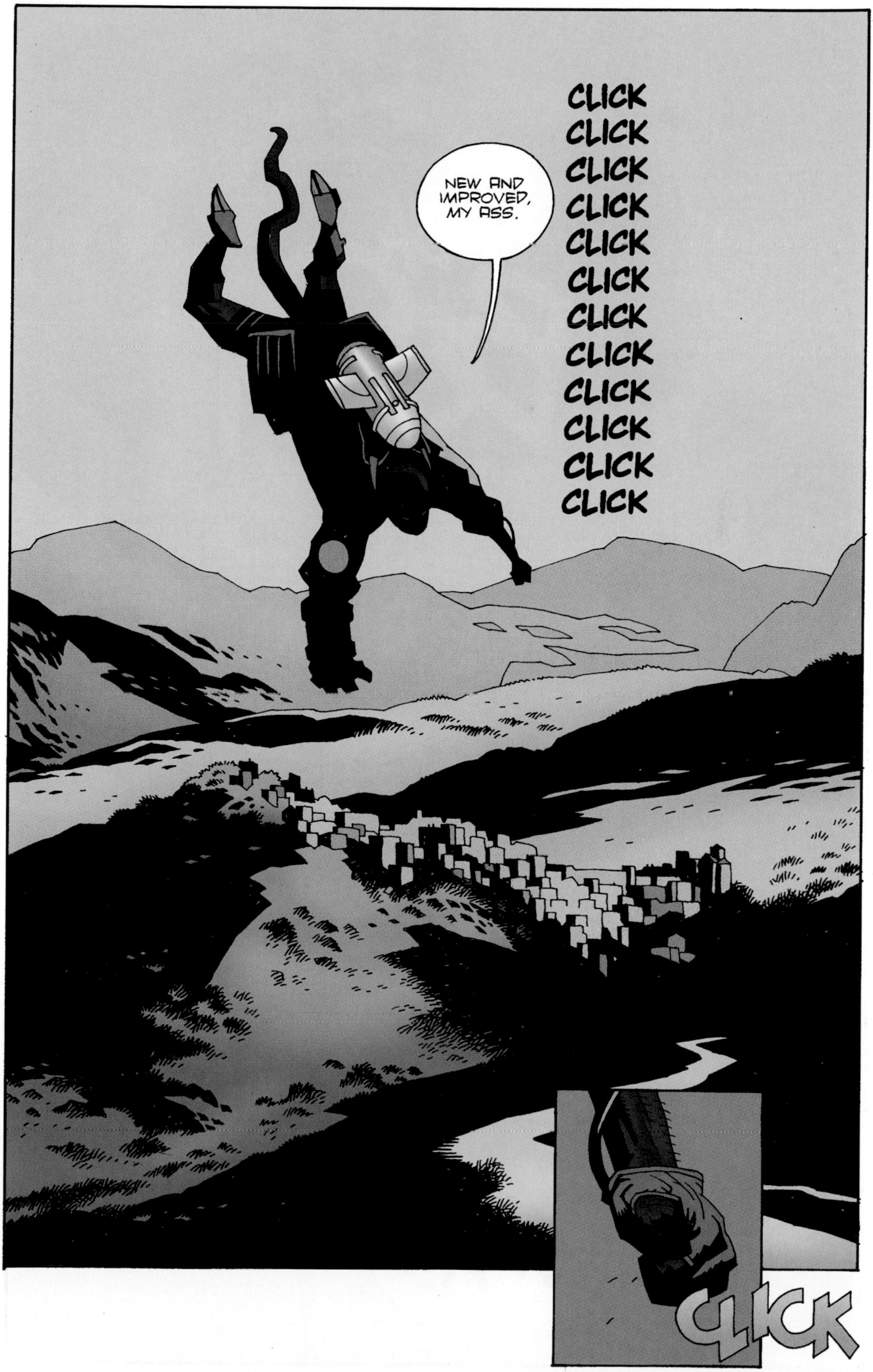

NEW AND IMPROVED, MY ASS.
CLICK
CLICK
CLICK
CLICK
CLICK
CLICK
CLICK
CLICK
CLICK
CLICK
CLICK
CLICK
CLICK

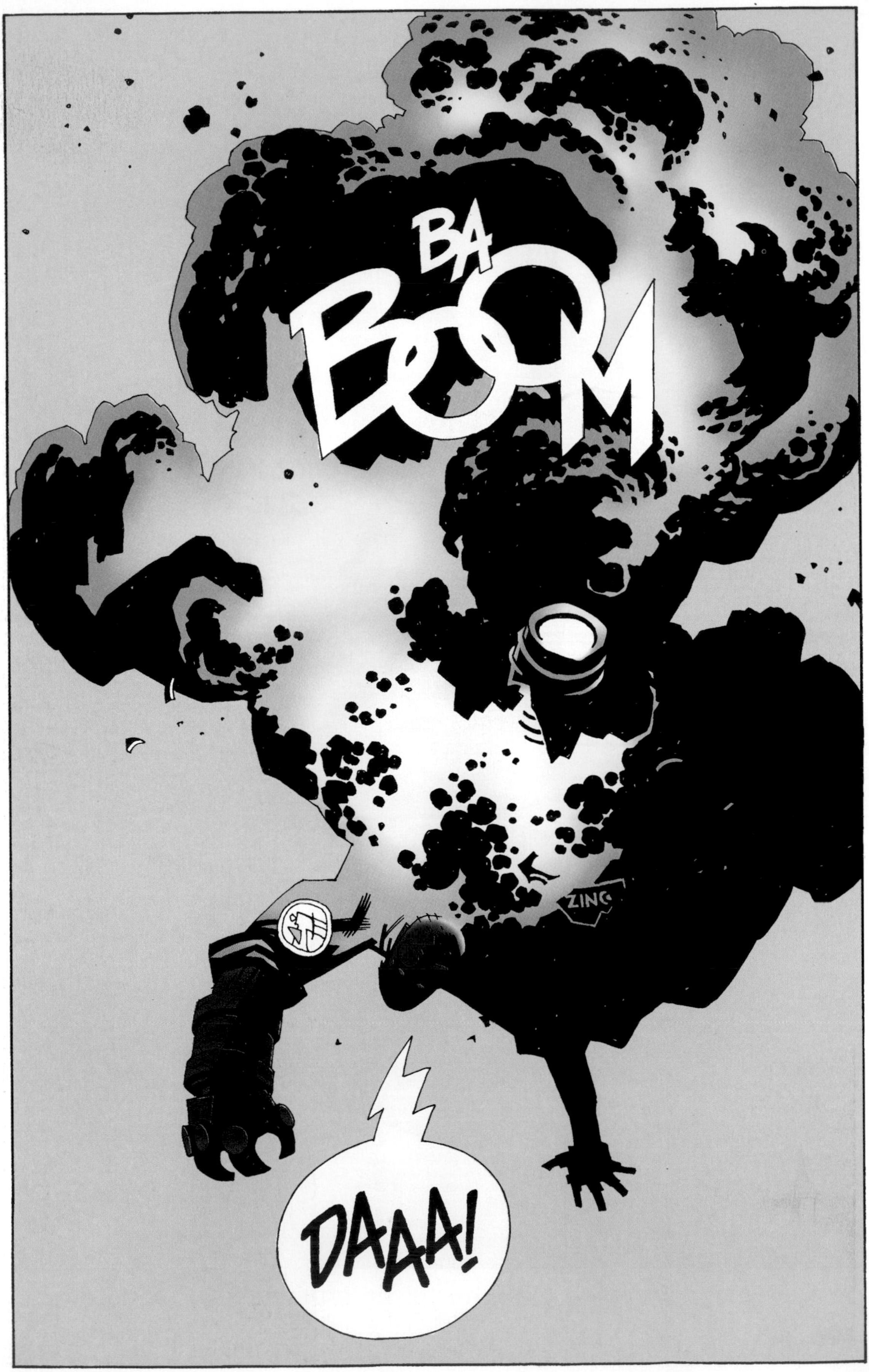
BA BOOM
ZING
DAAA!

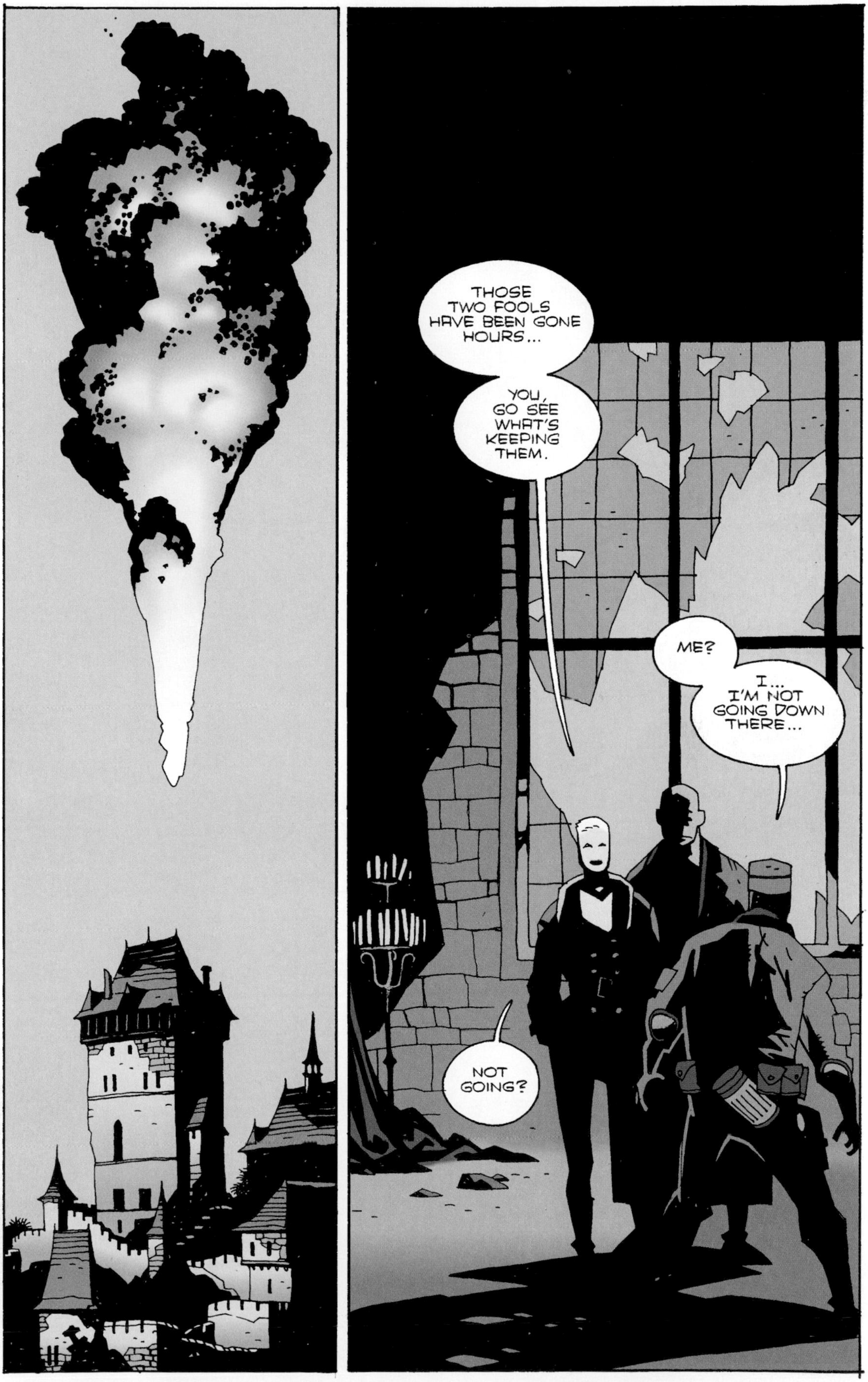
THOSE TWO FOOLS HAVE BEEN GONE HOURS...
YOU, GO SEE WHAT'S KEEPING THEM.
ME?
I... I'M NOT GOING DOWN THERE...
NOT GOING?

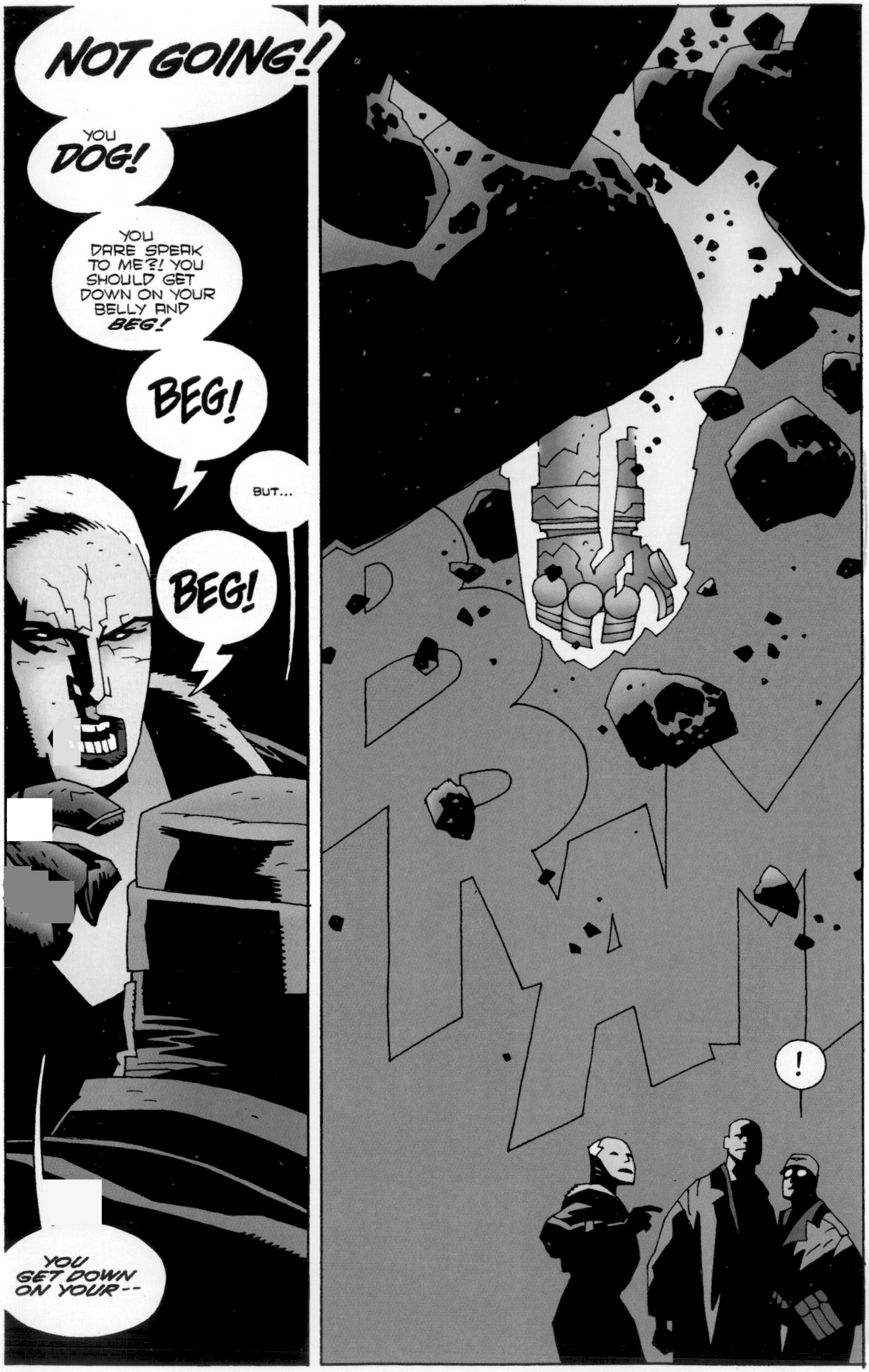
NOT GOING!
YOU DOG!
YOU DARE SPEAK TO ME?! YOU SHOULD GET DOWN ON YOUR BELLY AND BEG!
BEG!
BUT...
BEG!
YOU GET DOWN ON YOUR--
!

CHAPTER TWO

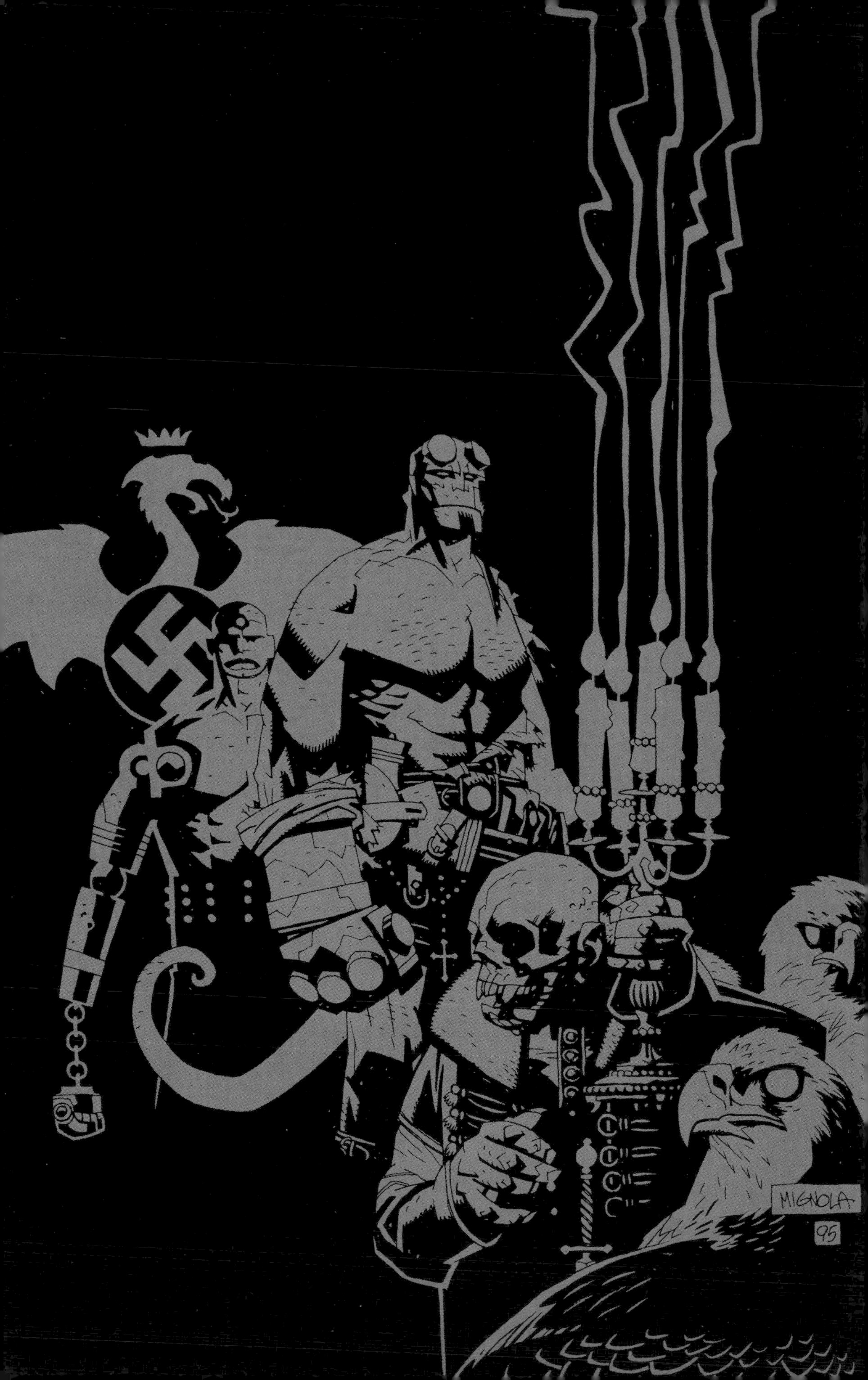
MIGNOLA
95

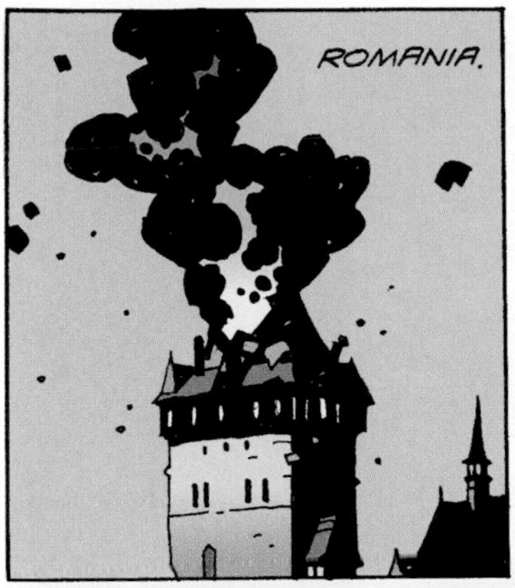
ROMANIA.

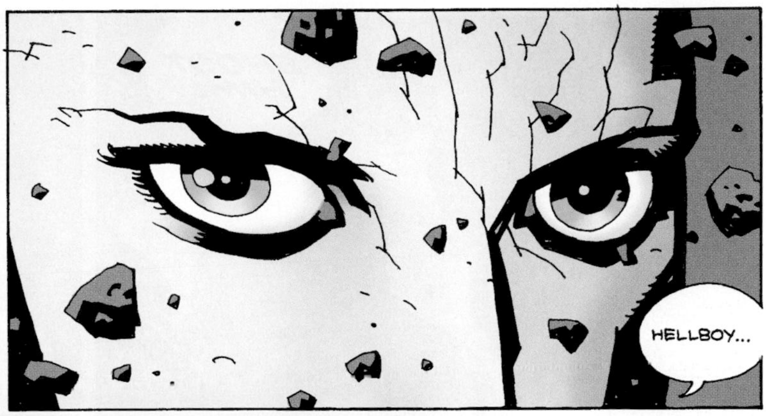
HELLBOY...

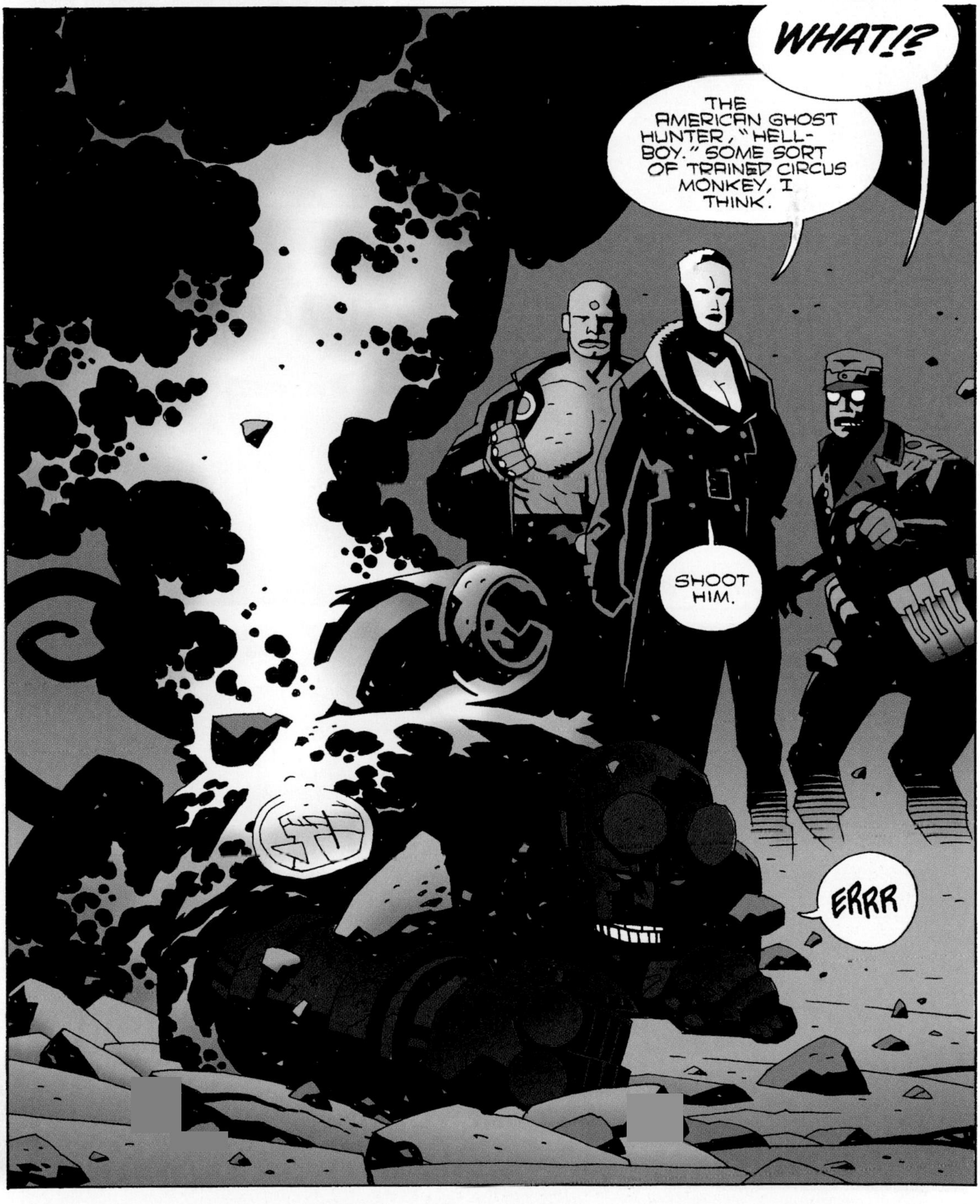
WHAT!?
THE AMERICAN GHOST HUNTER, "HELL-BOY." SOME SORT OF TRAINED CIRCUS MONKEY, I THINK.
SHOOT HIM.
ERRR

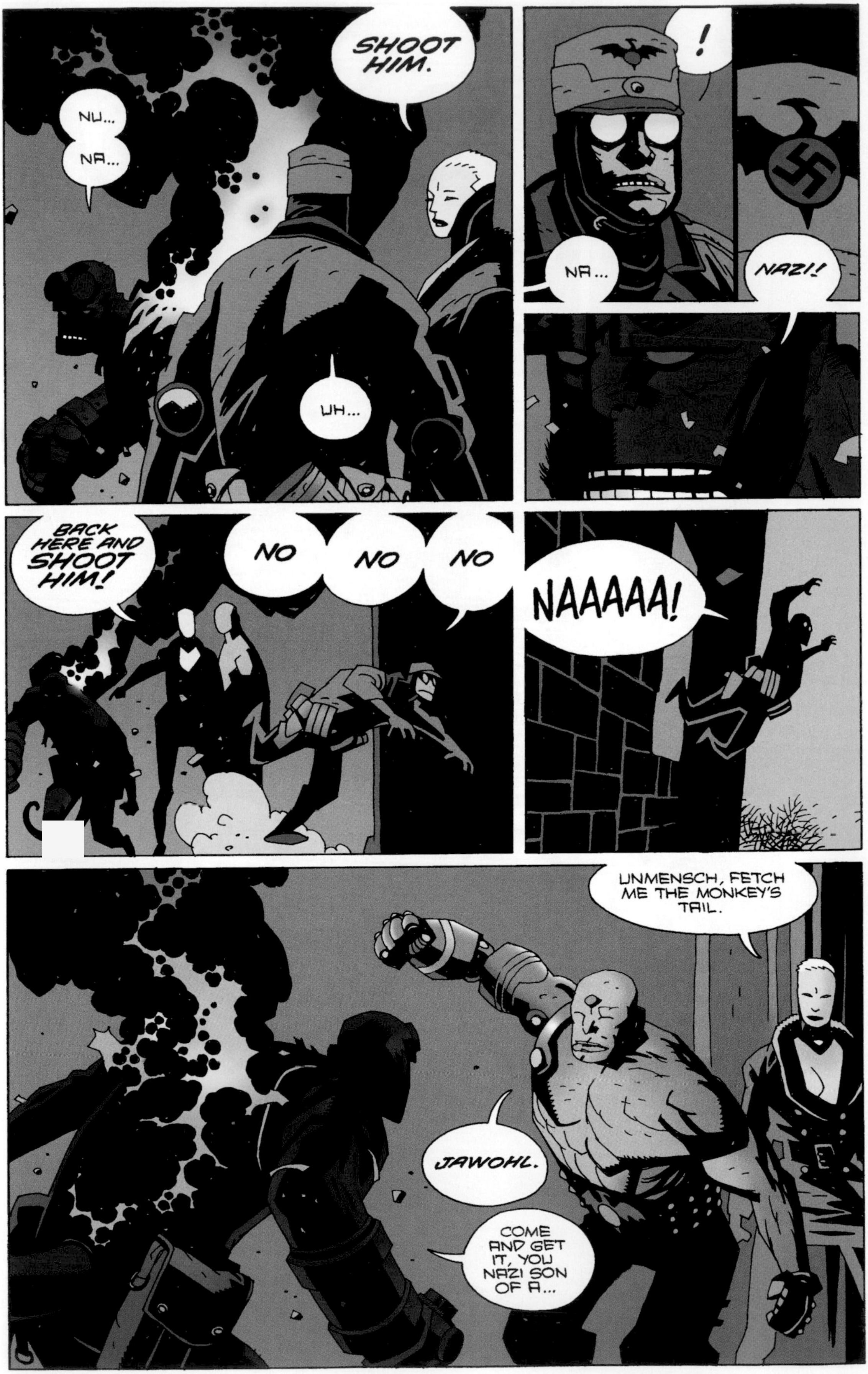
SHOOT HIM.
NU...
NA...
UH...
!
NA...
NAZI!
BACK HERE AND SHOOT HIM!
NO
NO
NO
NAAAAA!
UNMENSCH, FETCH ME THE MONKEY'S TAIL.
JAWOHL.
COME AND GET IT, YOU NAZI SON OF A...

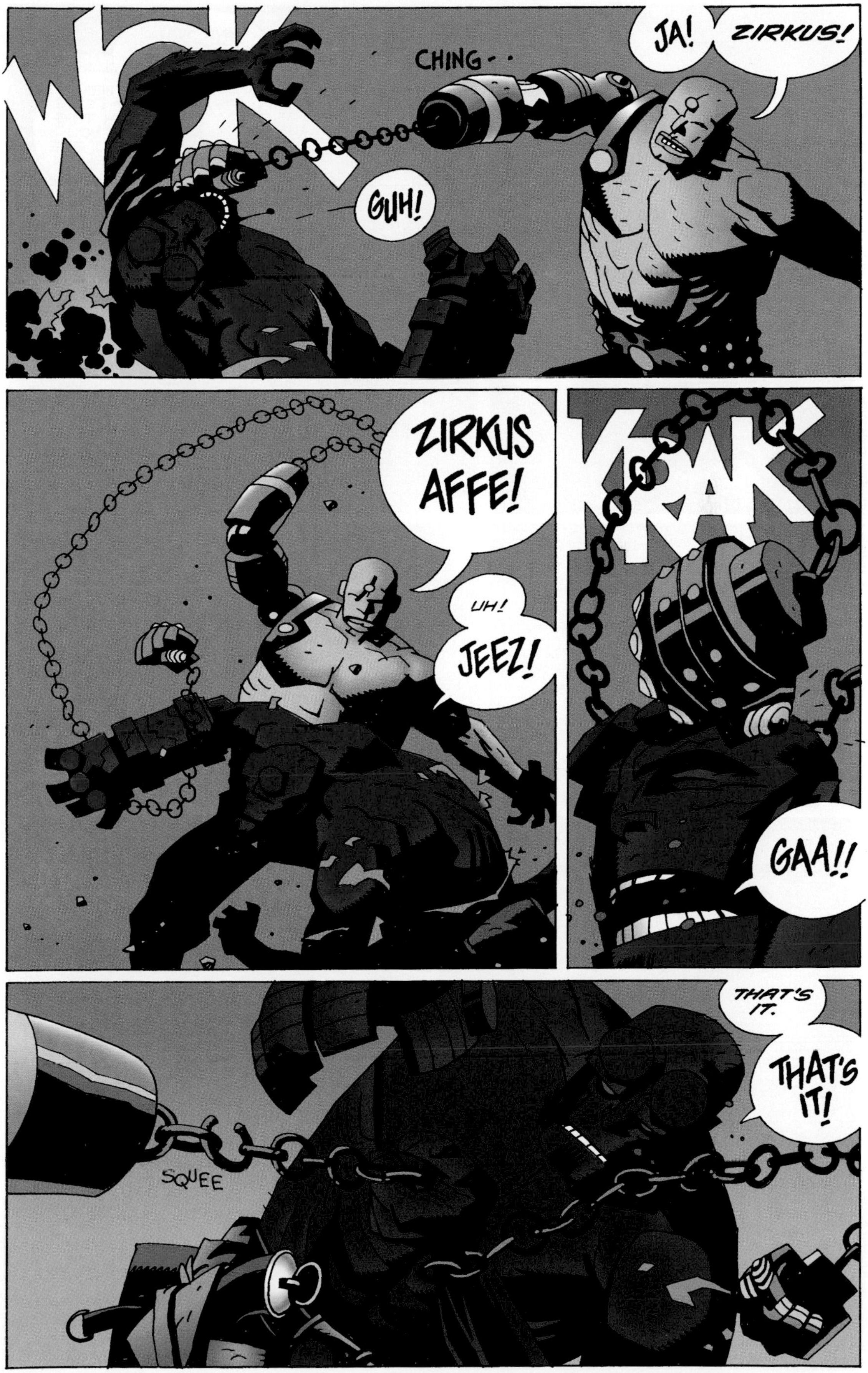

WOK
CHING- -
JA!
ZIRKUS!
GUH!
ZIRKUS AFFE!
UH!
JEEZ!
KRAK
GAA!!
THAT'S IT.
THAT'S IT!
SQUEE

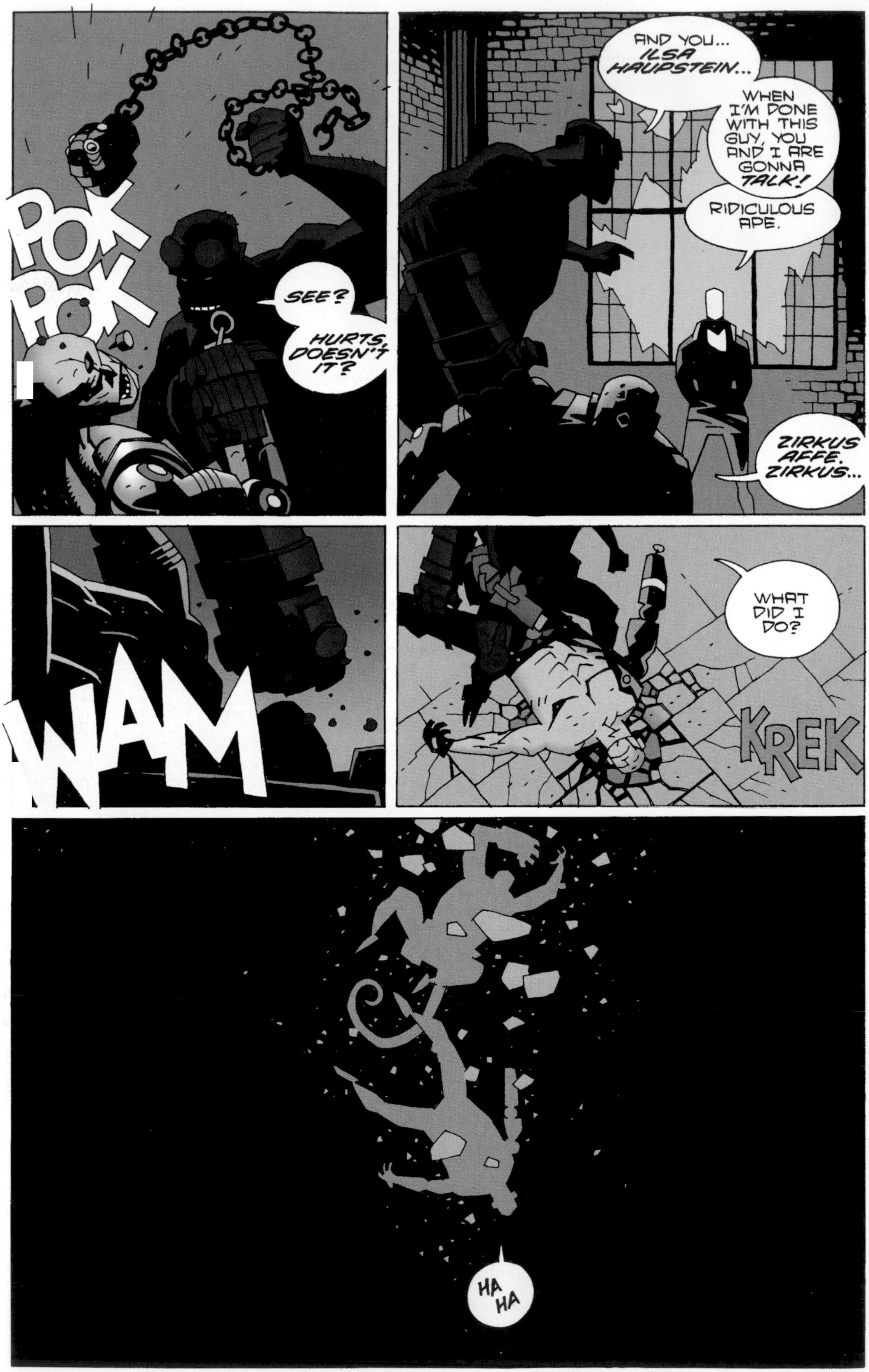
POK
POK
SEE?
HURTS, DOESN'T IT?
AND YOU... ILSA HAUPSTEIN...
WHEN I'M DONE WITH THIS GUY, YOU AND I ARE GONNA TALK!
RIDICULOUS APE.
ZIRKUS AFFE. ZIRKUS...
WAM
WHAT DID I DO?
KREK
HA HA

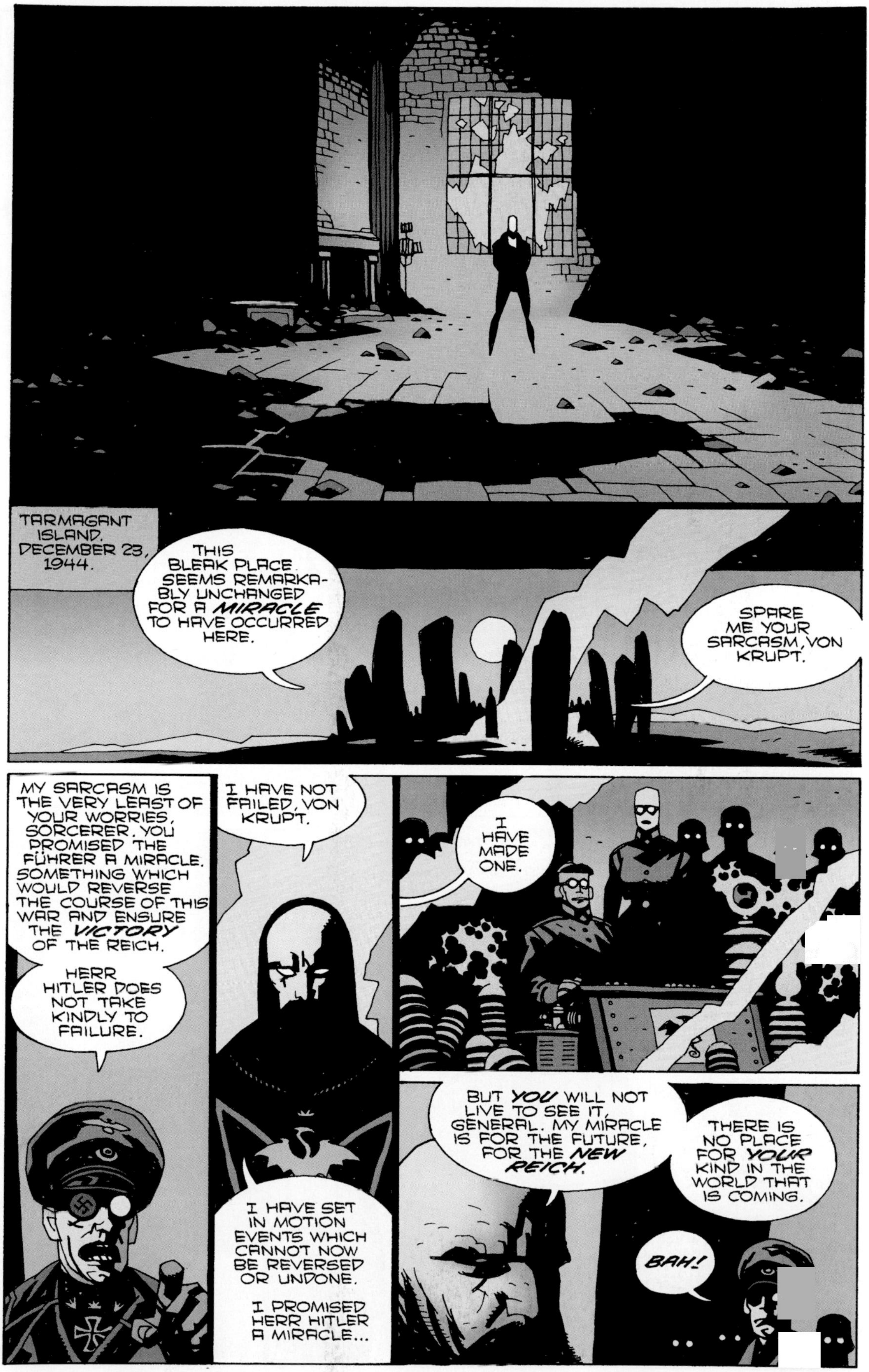

TARMAGANT ISLAND. DECEMBER 23, 1944.
THIS BLEAK PLACE SEEMS REMARKABLY UNCHANGED FOR A MIRACLE TO HAVE OCCURRED HERE.
SPARE ME YOUR SARCASM, VON KRUPT.
MY SARCASM IS THE VERY LEAST OF YOUR WORRIES, SORCERER. YOU PROMISED THE FÜHRER A MIRACLE. SOMETHING WHICH WOULD REVERSE THE COURSE OF THIS WAR AND ENSURE THE VICTORY OF THE REICH.
HERR HITLER DOES NOT TAKE KINDLY TO FAILURE.
I HAVE NOT FAILED, VON KRUPT.
I HAVE SET IN MOTION EVENTS WHICH CANNOT NOW BE REVERSED OR UNDONE.
I PROMISED HERR HITLER A MIRACLE...
I HAVE MADE ONE.
BUT YOU WILL NOT LIVE TO SEE IT, GENERAL. MY MIRACLE IS FOR THE FUTURE, FOR THE NEW REICH.
THERE IS NO PLACE FOR YOUR KIND IN THE WORLD THAT IS COMING.
BAH!

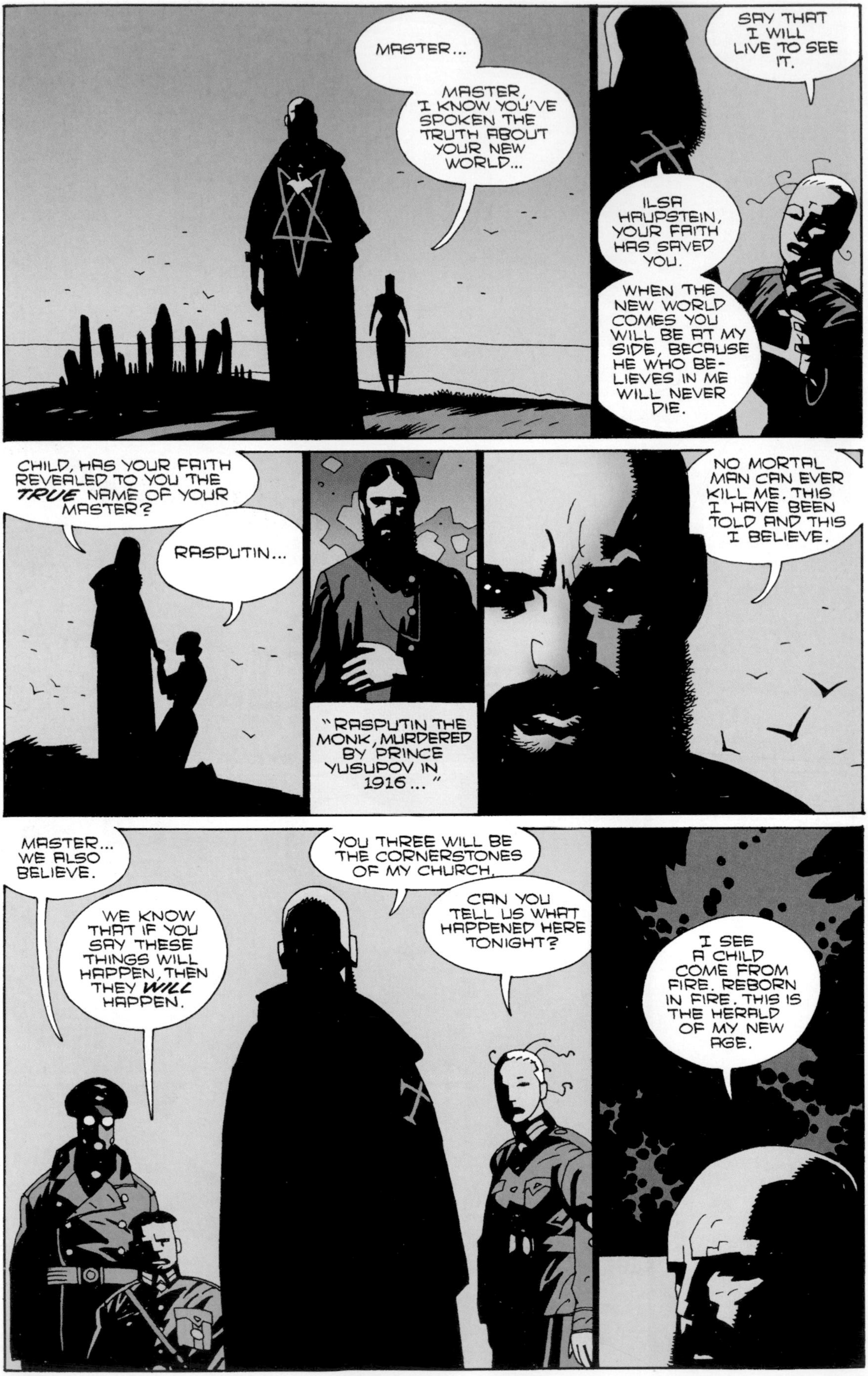
MASTER...
MASTER, I KNOW YOU'VE SPOKEN THE TRUTH ABOUT YOUR NEW WORLD...
SAY THAT I WILL LIVE TO SEE IT.
ILSA HAUPSTEIN, YOUR FAITH HAS SAVED YOU.
WHEN THE NEW WORLD COMES YOU WILL BE AT MY SIDE, BECAUSE HE WHO BE- LIEVES IN ME WILL NEVER DIE.
CHILD, HAS YOUR FAITH REVEALED TO YOU THE TRUE NAME OF YOUR MASTER?
RASPUTIN...
"RASPUTIN THE MONK, MURDERED BY PRINCE YUSUPOV IN 1916..."
NO MORTAL MAN CAN EVER KILL ME. THIS I HAVE BEEN TOLD AND THIS I BELIEVE.
MASTER... WE ALSO BELIEVE.
WE KNOW THAT IF YOU SAY THESE THINGS WILL HAPPEN, THEN THEY WILL HAPPEN.
YOU THREE WILL BE THE CORNERSTONES OF MY CHURCH.
CAN YOU TELL US WHAT HAPPENED HERE TONIGHT?
I SEE A CHILD COME FROM FIRE. REBORN IN FIRE. THIS IS THE HERALD OF MY NEW AGE.

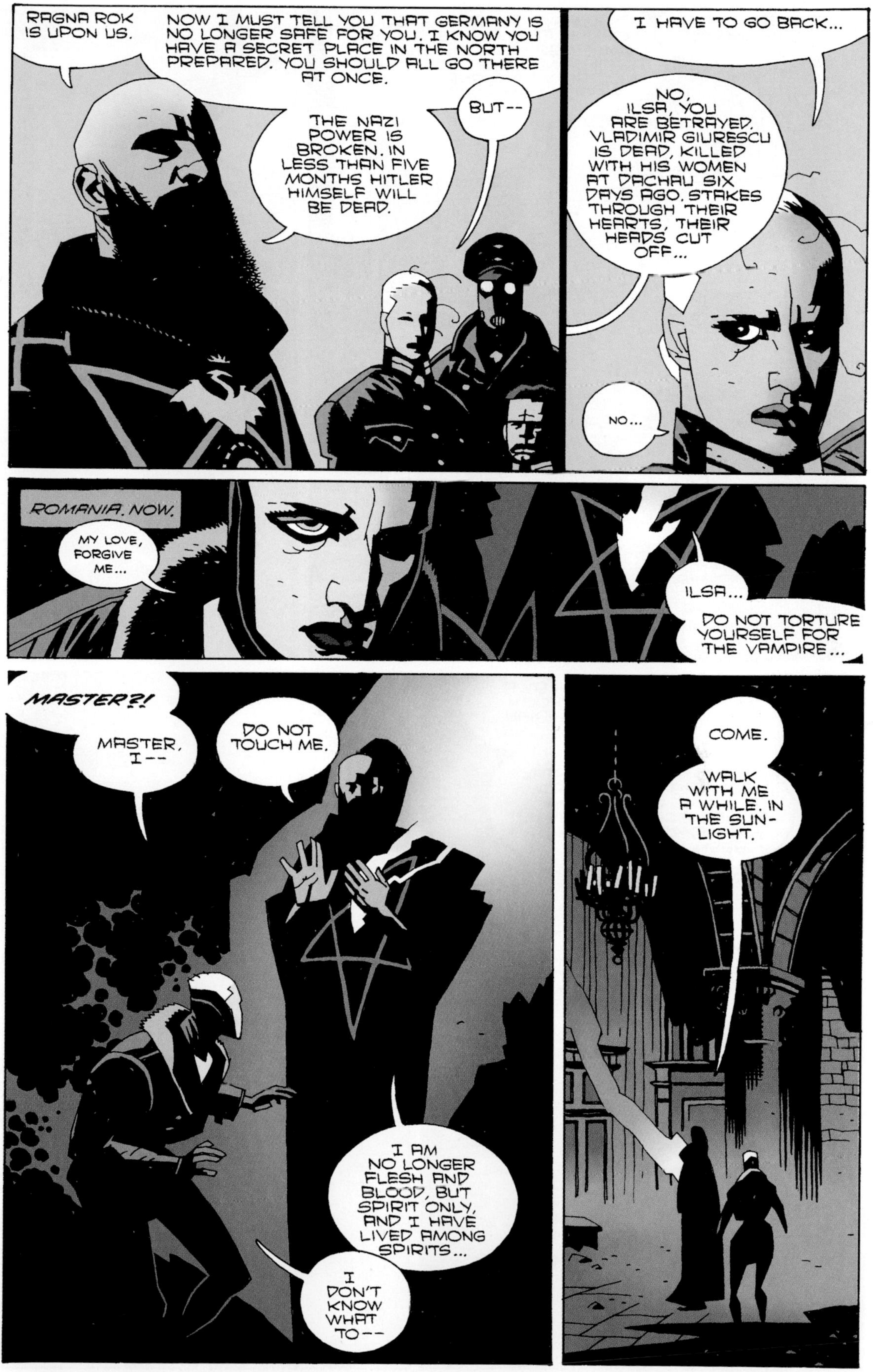
RAGNA ROK IS UPON US.
NOW I MUST TELL YOU THAT GERMANY IS NO LONGER SAFE FOR YOU. I KNOW YOU HAVE A SECRET PLACE IN THE NORTH PREPARED. YOU SHOULD ALL GO THERE AT ONCE.
BUT--
THE NAZI POWER IS BROKEN. IN LESS THAN FIVE MONTHS HITLER HIMSELF WILL BE DEAD.
I HAVE TO GO BACK...
NO, ILSA, YOU ARE BETRAYED. VLADIMIR GIURESCU IS DEAD, KILLED WITH HIS WOMEN AT DACHAU SIX DAYS AGO. STAKES THROUGH THEIR HEARTS, THEIR HEADS CUT OFF...
NO...
ROMANIA. NOW.
MY LOVE, FORGIVE ME...
ILSA...
DO NOT TORTURE YOURSELF FOR THE VAMPIRE...
MASTER?!
MASTER, I--
DO NOT TOUCH ME.
I AM NO LONGER FLESH AND BLOOD, BUT SPIRIT ONLY, AND I HAVE LIVED AMONG SPIRITS...
I DON'T KNOW WHAT TO--
COME.
WALK WITH ME A WHILE. IN THE SUN-LIGHT.

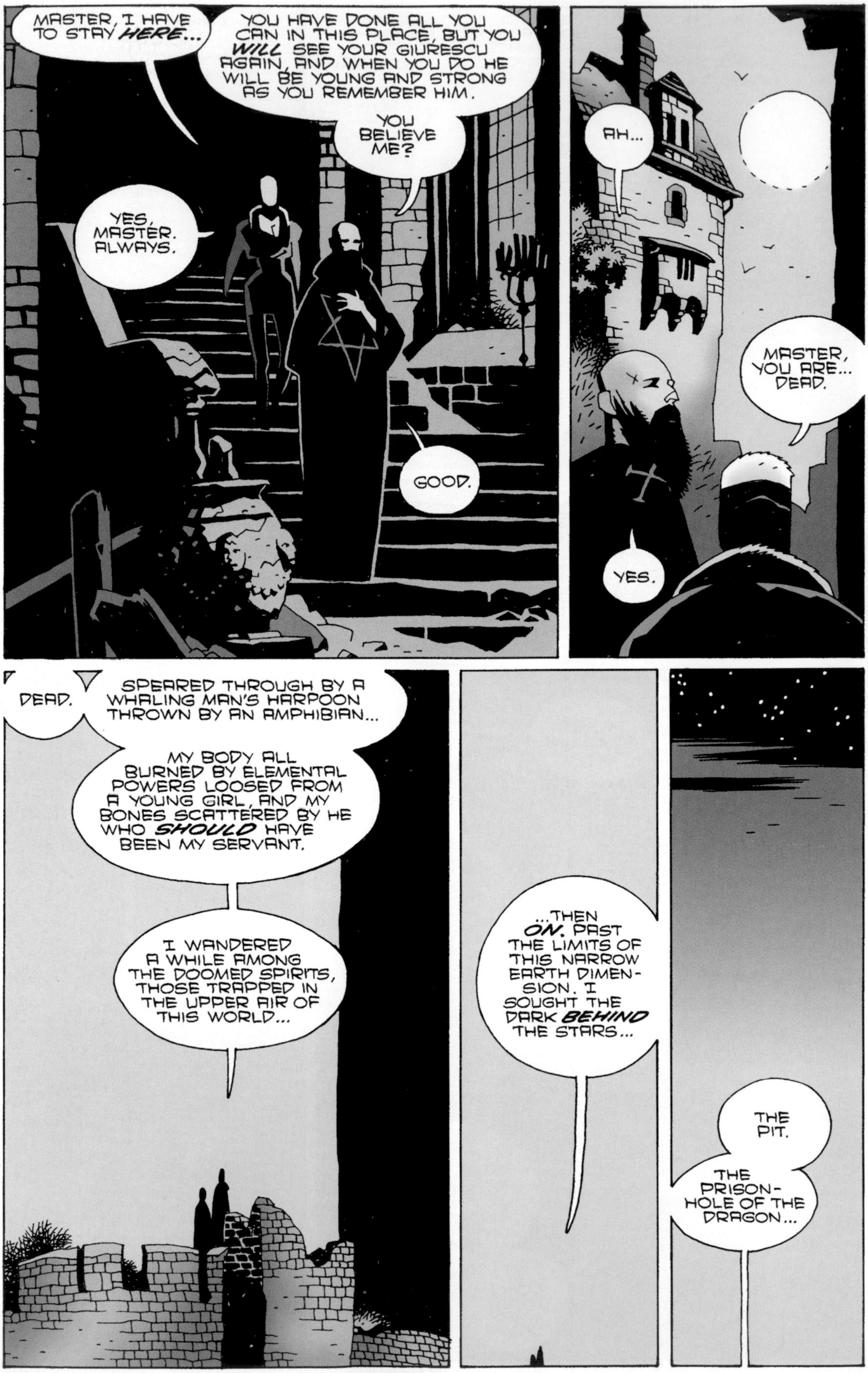
MASTER, I HAVE TO STAY HERE...
YOU HAVE DONE ALL YOU CAN IN THIS PLACE, BUT YOU WILL SEE YOUR GIURESCU AGAIN, AND WHEN YOU DO HE WILL BE YOUNG AND STRONG AS YOU REMEMBER HIM.
YOU BELIEVE ME?
YES, MASTER. ALWAYS.
GOOD.
AH...
MASTER, YOU ARE... DEAD.
YES.
DEAD.
SPEARED THROUGH BY A WHALING MAN'S HARPOON THROWN BY AN AMPHIBIAN...
MY BODY ALL BURNED BY ELEMENTAL POWERS LOOSED FROM A YOUNG GIRL, AND MY BONES SCATTERED BY HE WHO SHOULD HAVE BEEN MY SERVANT.
I WANDERED A WHILE AMONG THE DOOMED SPIRITS, THOSE TRAPPED IN THE UPPER AIR OF THIS WORLD...
...THEN ON. PAST THE LIMITS OF THIS NARROW EARTH DIMENSION. I SOUGHT THE DARK BEHIND THE STARS...
THE PIT.
THE PRISON-HOLE OF THE DRAGON...

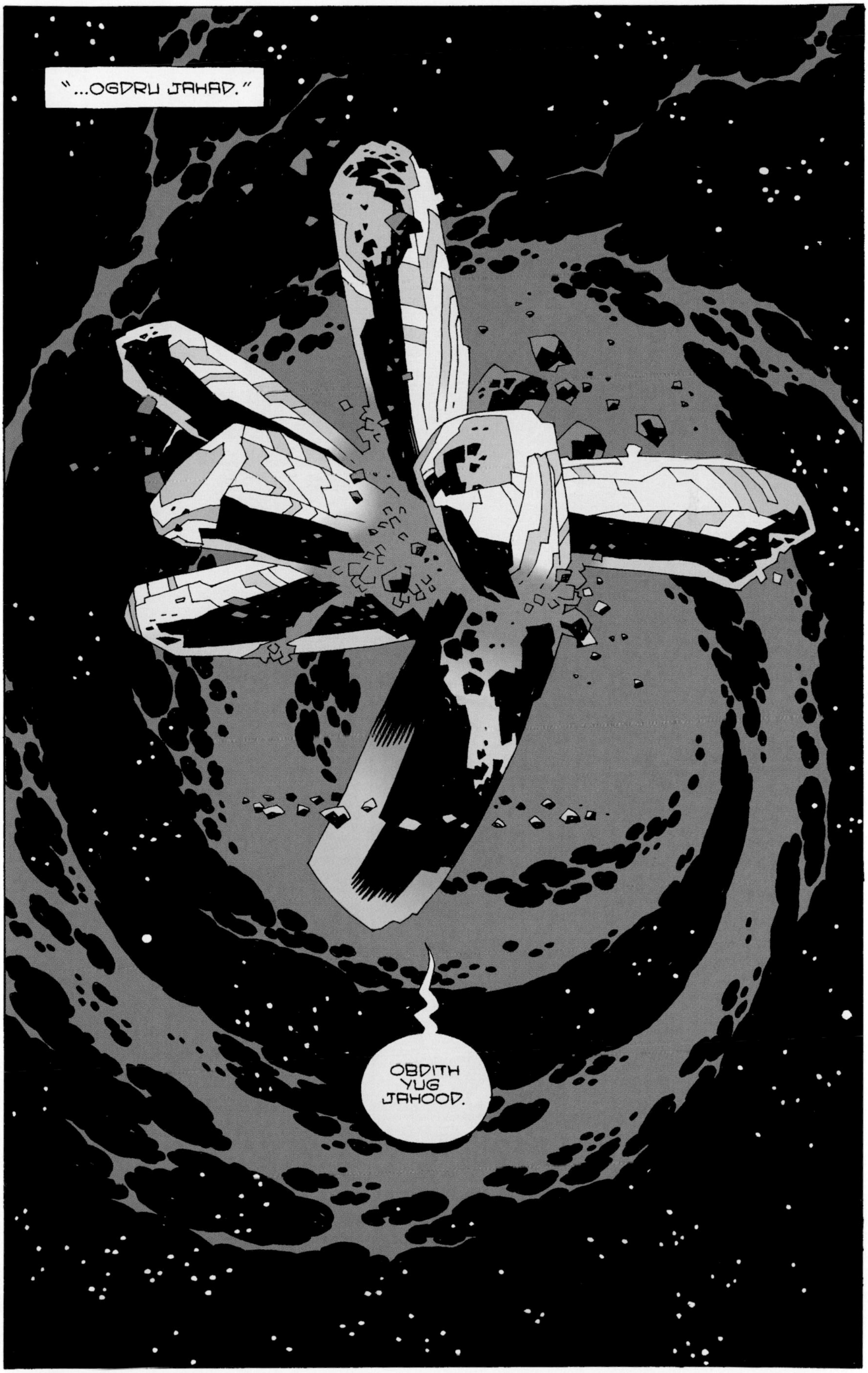
"...OGDRU JAHAD."
OBDITH YUG JAHOOD.

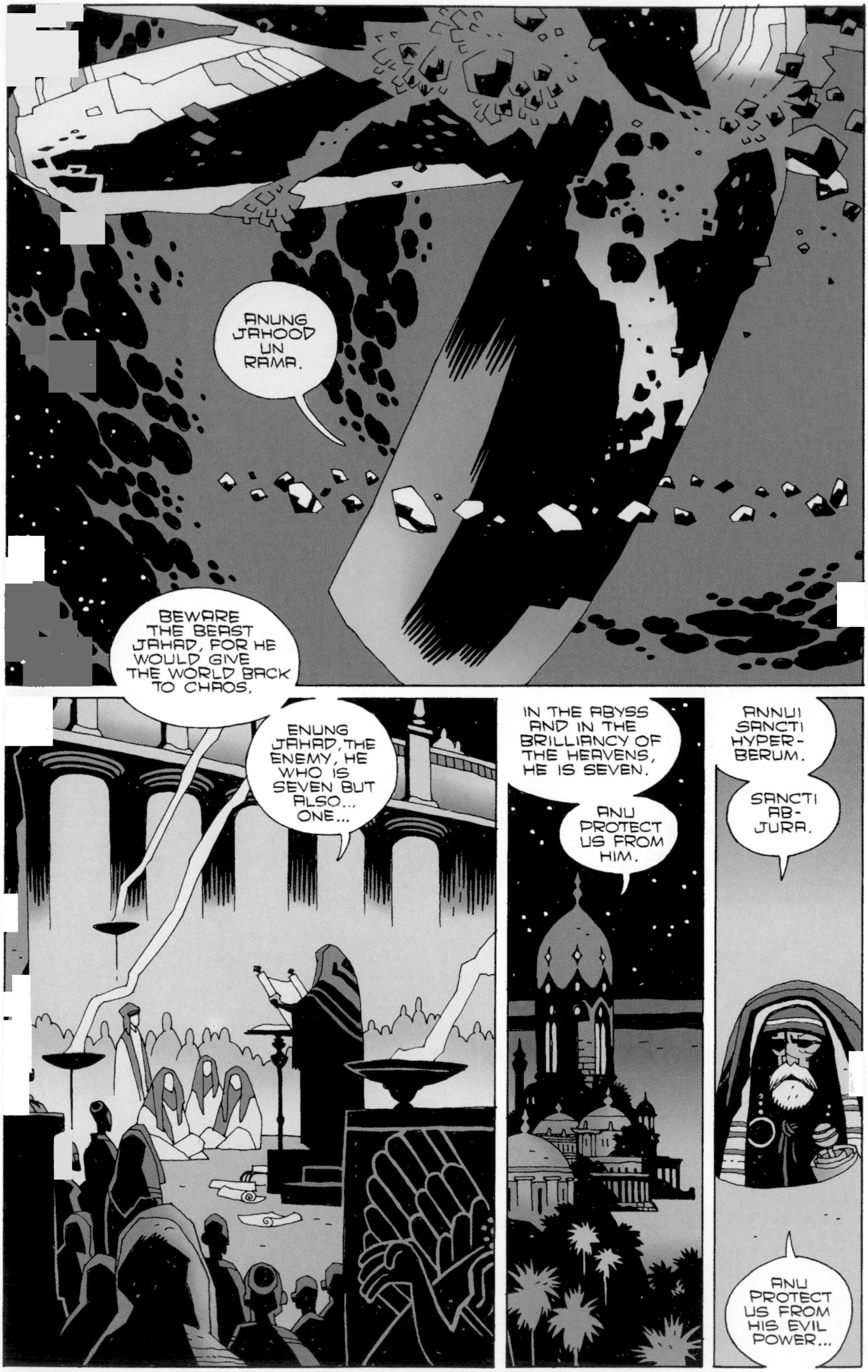
ANUNG JAHOOD UN RAMA.
BEWARE THE BEAST JAHAD, FOR HE WOULD GIVE THE WORLD BACK TO CHAOS.
ENUNG JAHAD, THE ENEMY, HE WHO IS SEVEN BUT ALSO... ONE...
IN THE ABYSS AND IN THE BRILLIANCY OF THE HEAVENS, HE IS SEVEN.
ANU PROTECT US FROM HIM.
ANNUI SANCTI HYPER-BERUM.
SANCTI AB-JURA.
ANU PROTECT US FROM HIS EVIL POWER...

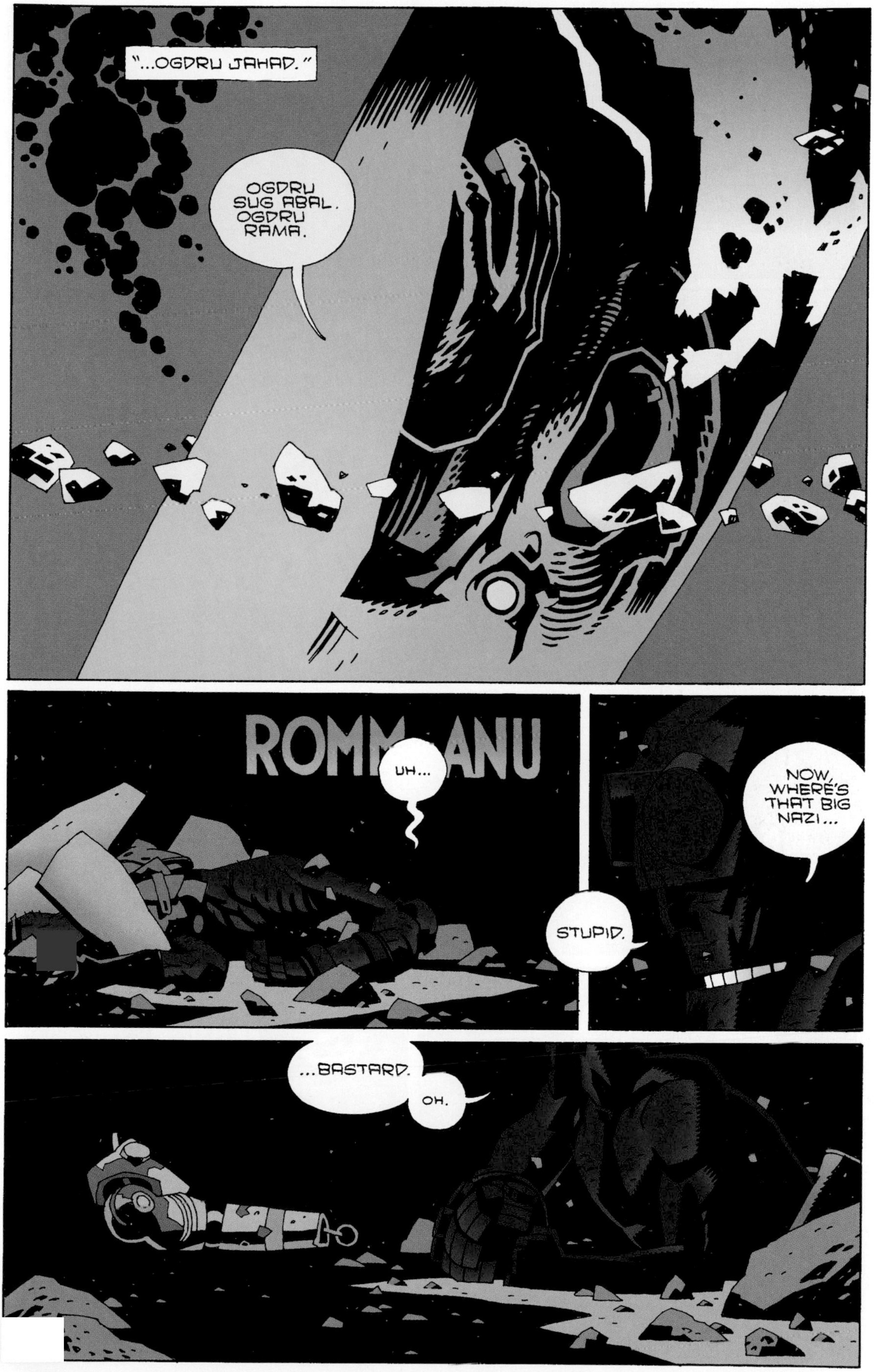
"...OGDRU JAHAD."
OGDRU SUG ABAL. OGDRU RAMA.
ROMM ANU
UH...
NOW, WHERE'S THAT BIG NAZI...
STUPID.
...BASTARD.
OH.

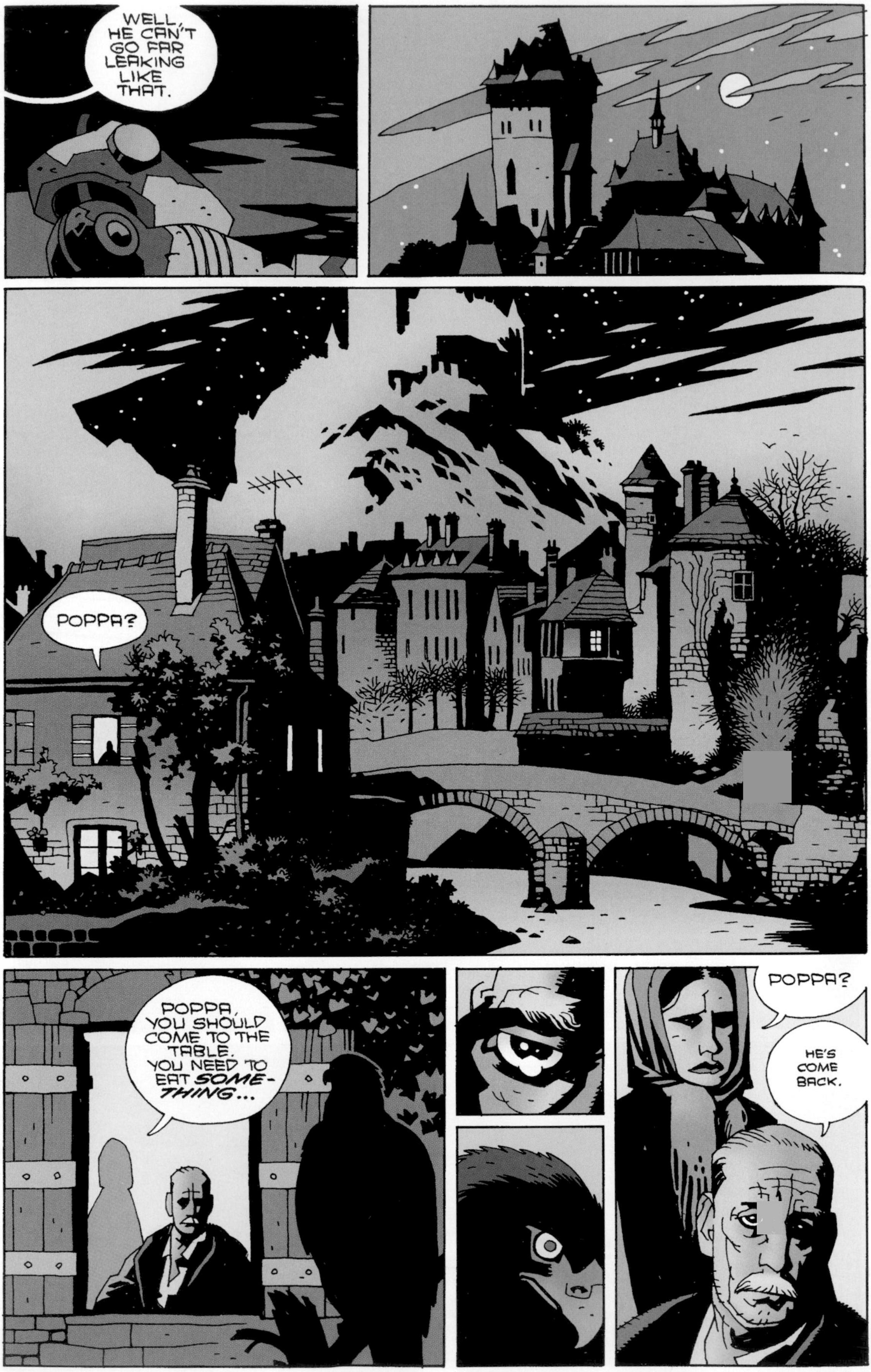
WELL, HE CAN'T GO FAR LEAKING LIKE THAT.
POPPA?
POPPA, YOU SHOULD COME TO THE TABLE. YOU NEED TO EAT *SOMETHING*...
POPPA?
HE'S COME BACK.

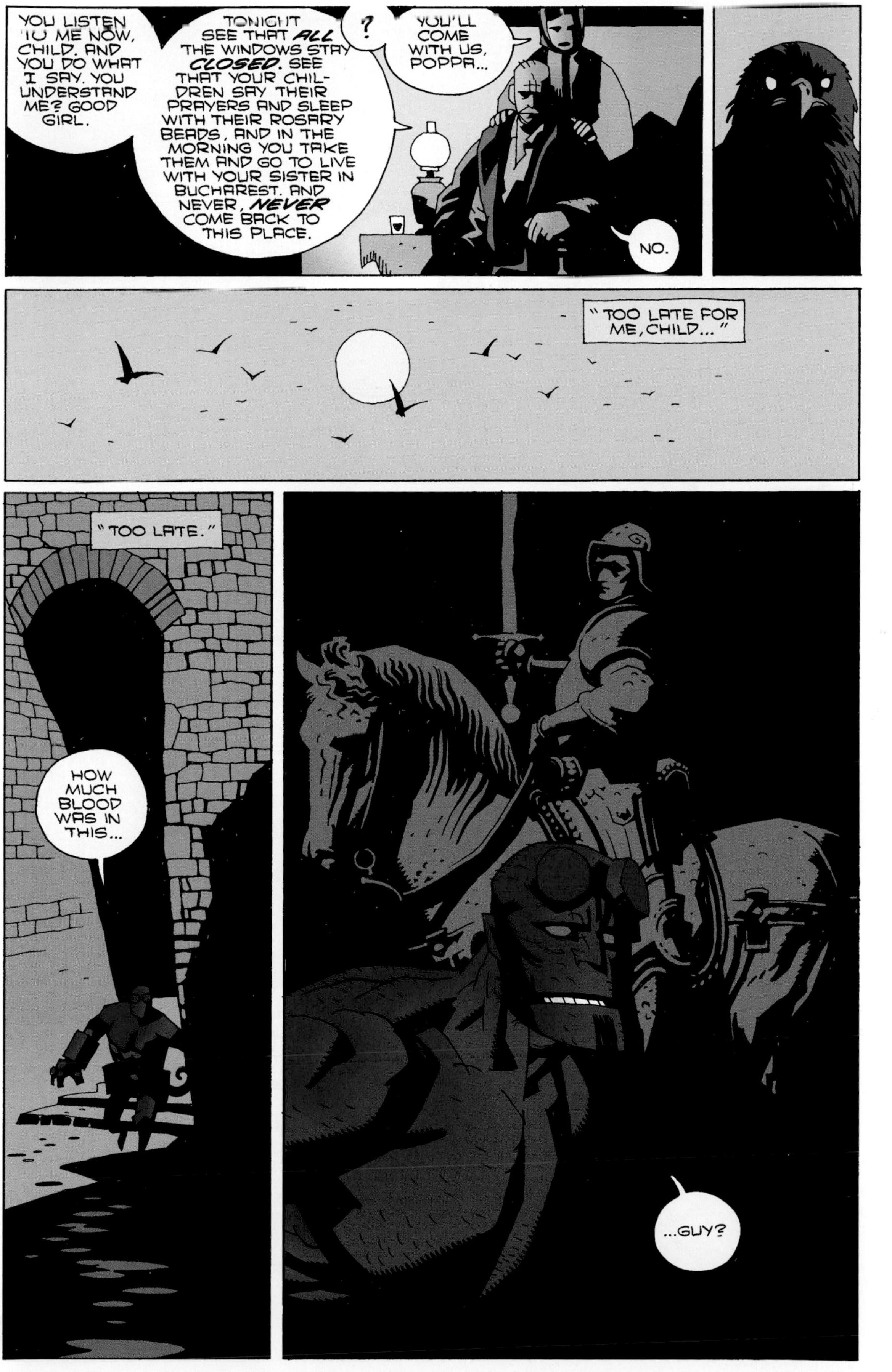
YOU LISTEN TO ME NOW, CHILD. AND YOU DO WHAT I SAY. YOU UNDERSTAND ME? GOOD GIRL.
TONIGHT SEE THAT ALL THE WINDOWS STAY CLOSED. SEE THAT YOUR CHILDREN SAY THEIR PRAYERS AND SLEEP WITH THEIR ROSARY BEADS, AND IN THE MORNING YOU TAKE THEM AND GO TO LIVE WITH YOUR SISTER IN BUCHAREST. AND NEVER, NEVER COME BACK TO THIS PLACE.
?
YOU'LL COME WITH US, POPPA...
NO.
"TOO LATE FOR ME, CHILD..."
"TOO LATE."
HOW MUCH BLOOD WAS IN THIS...
...GUY?

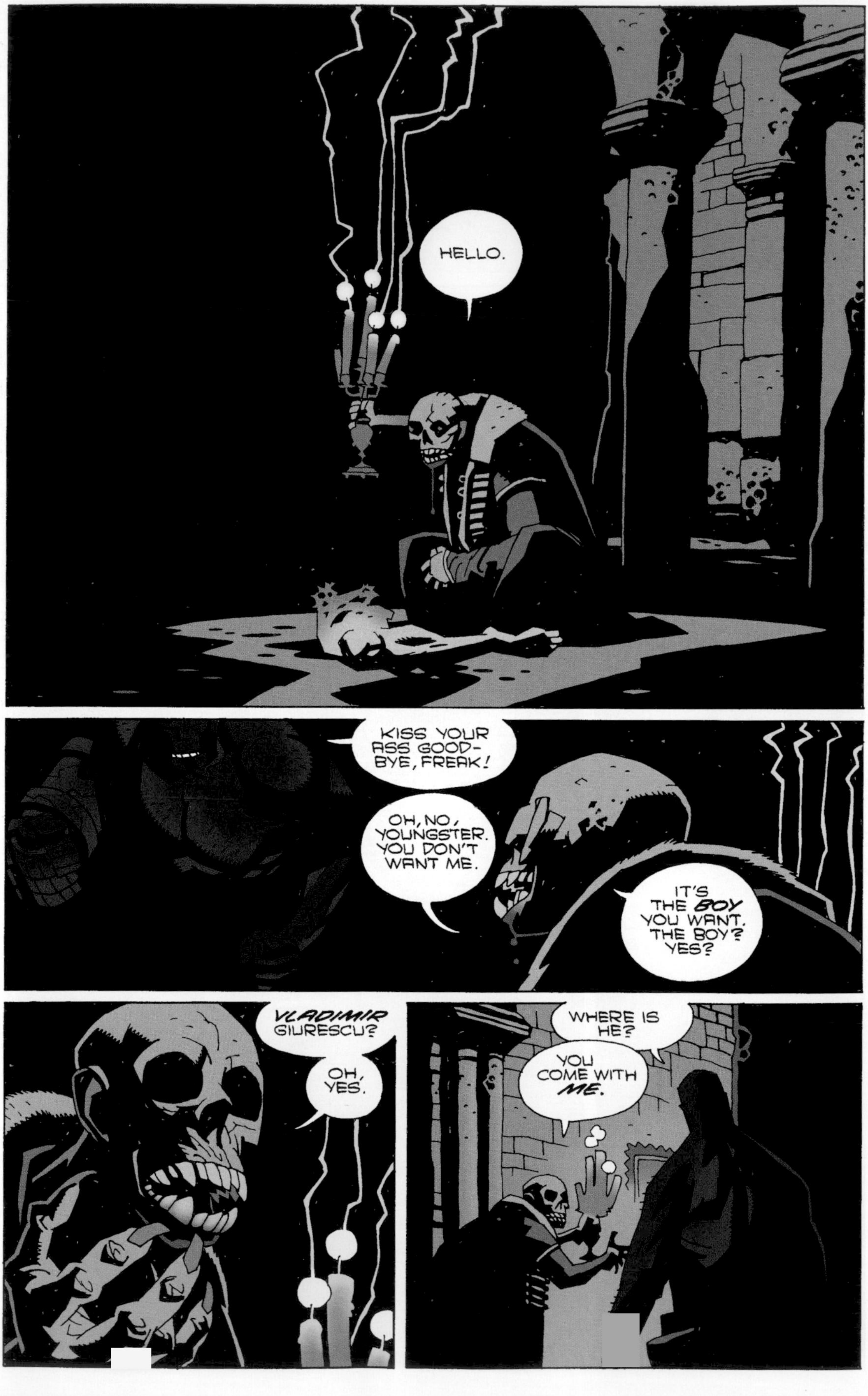
HELLO.
KISS YOUR ASS GOOD-BYE, FREAK!
OH, NO, YOUNGSTER. YOU DON'T WANT ME.
IT'S THE BOY YOU WANT. THE BOY? YES?
VLADIMIR GIURESCU?
OH, YES.
WHERE IS HE?
YOU COME WITH ME.

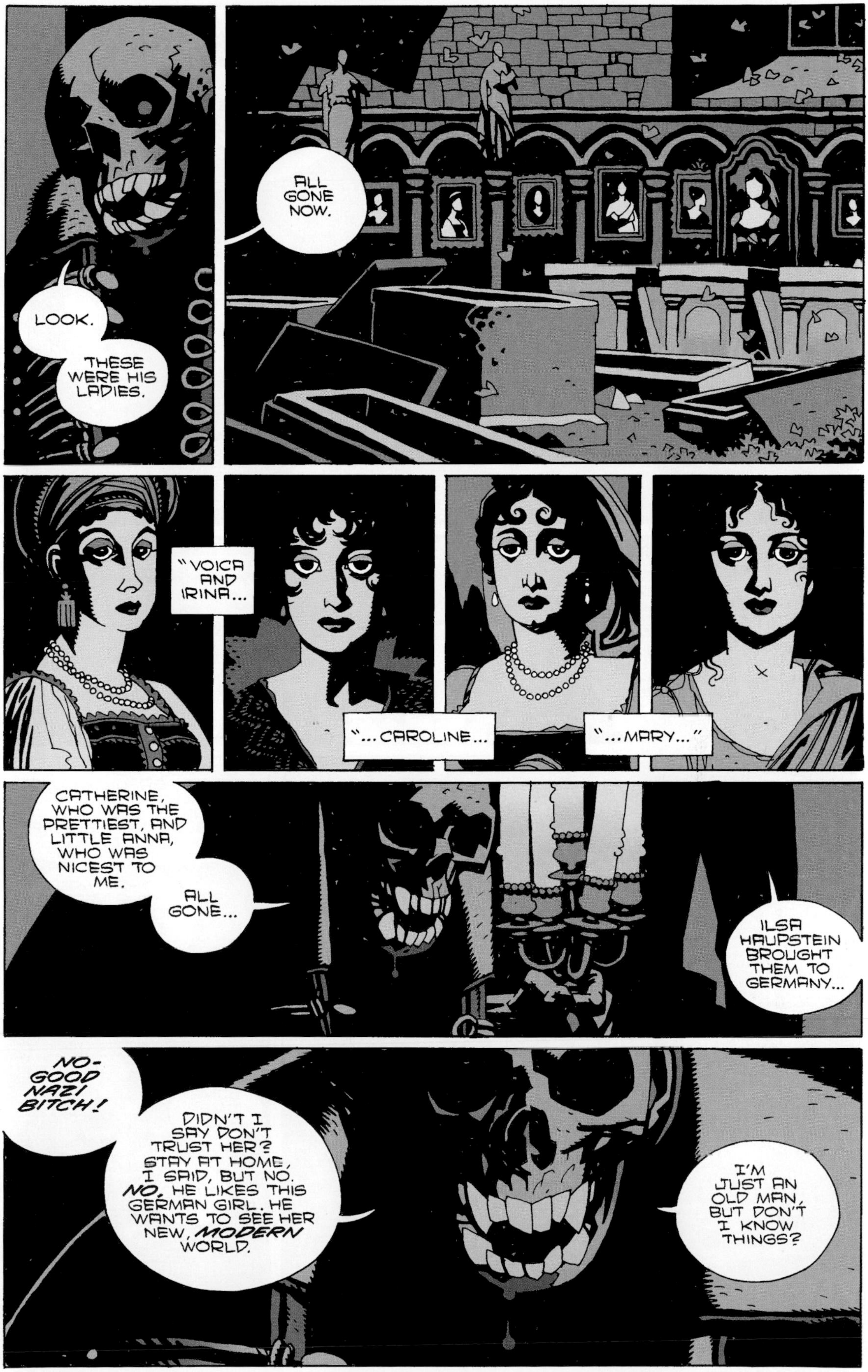
LOOK.
THESE WERE HIS LADIES.
ALL GONE NOW.
"VOICA AND IRINA...
"...CAROLINE...
"...MARY..."
CATHERINE, WHO WAS THE PRETTIEST, AND LITTLE ANNA, WHO WAS NICEST TO ME.
ALL GONE...
ILSA HAUPSTEIN BROUGHT THEM TO GERMANY...
NO-GOOD NAZI BITCH!
DIDN'T I SAY DON'T TRUST HER? STAY AT HOME, I SAID, BUT NO. NO. HE LIKES THIS GERMAN GIRL. HE WANTS TO SEE HER NEW, MODERN WORLD.
I'M JUST AN OLD MAN, BUT DON'T I KNOW THINGS?

*1492

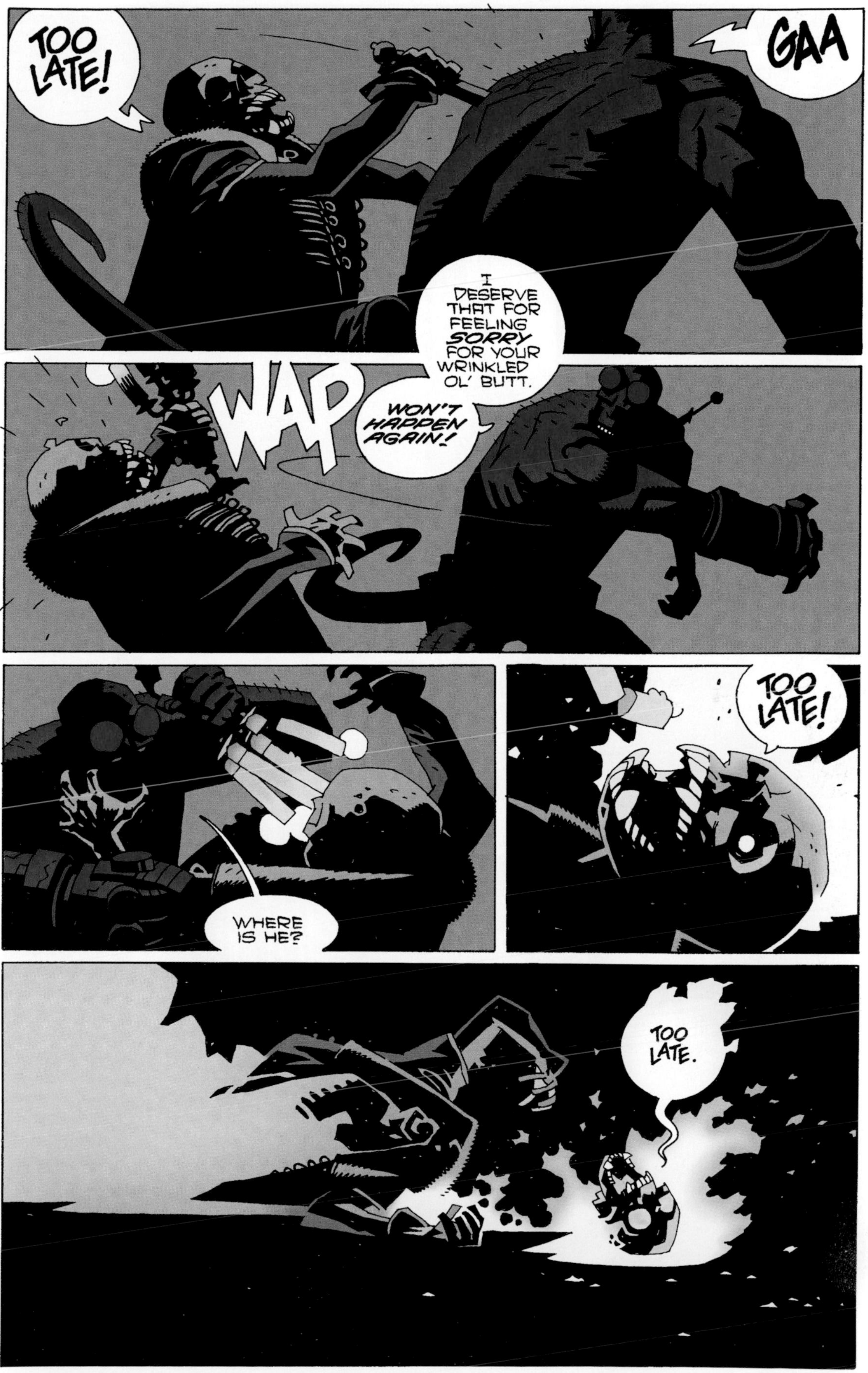
TOO LATE!
GAA
I DESERVE THAT FOR FEELING SORRY FOR YOUR WRINKLED OL' BUTT.
WAP
WON'T HAPPEN AGAIN!
WHERE IS HE?
TOO LATE!
TOO LATE.

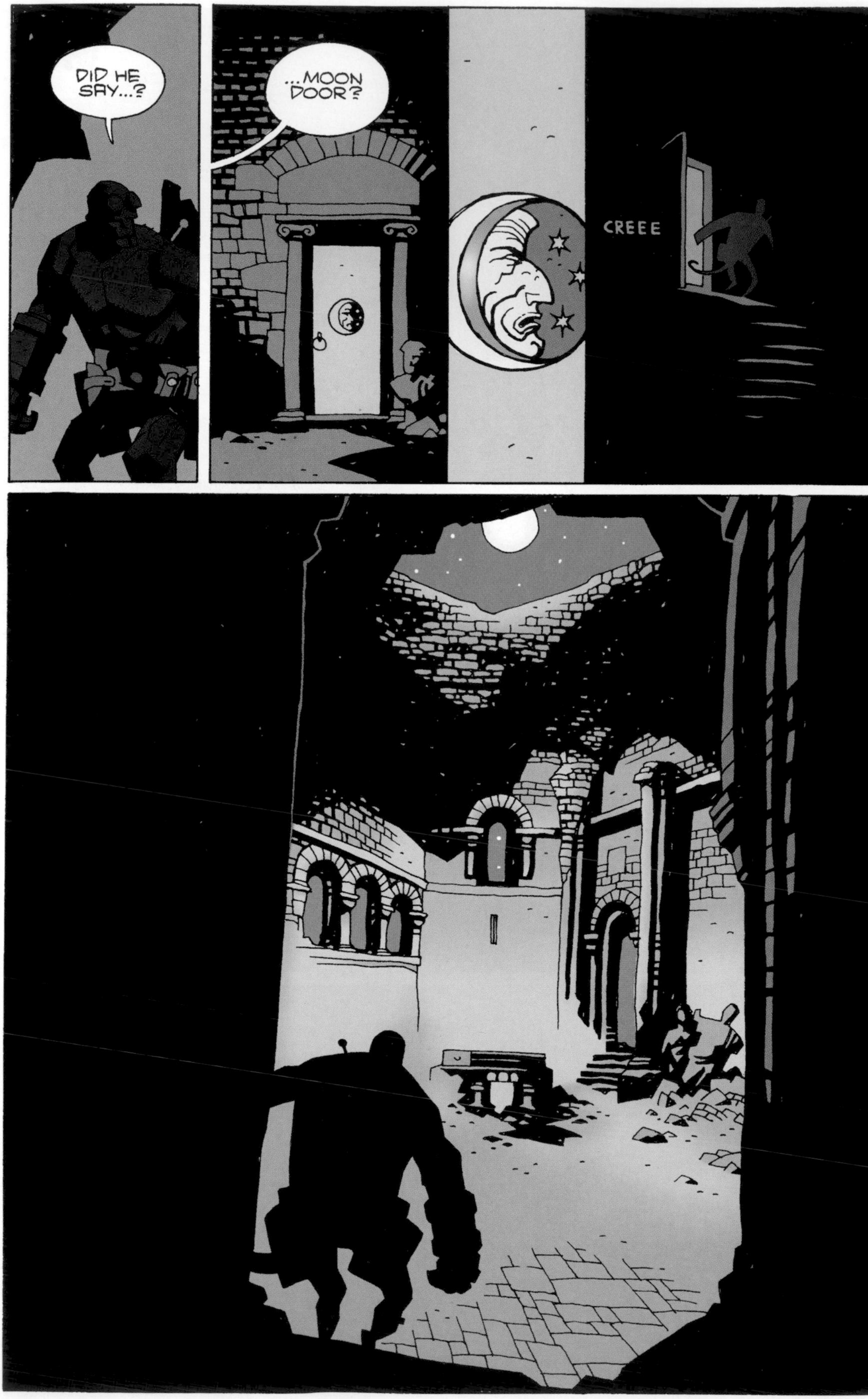
DID HE SAY...?
...MOON DOOR?
CREEE

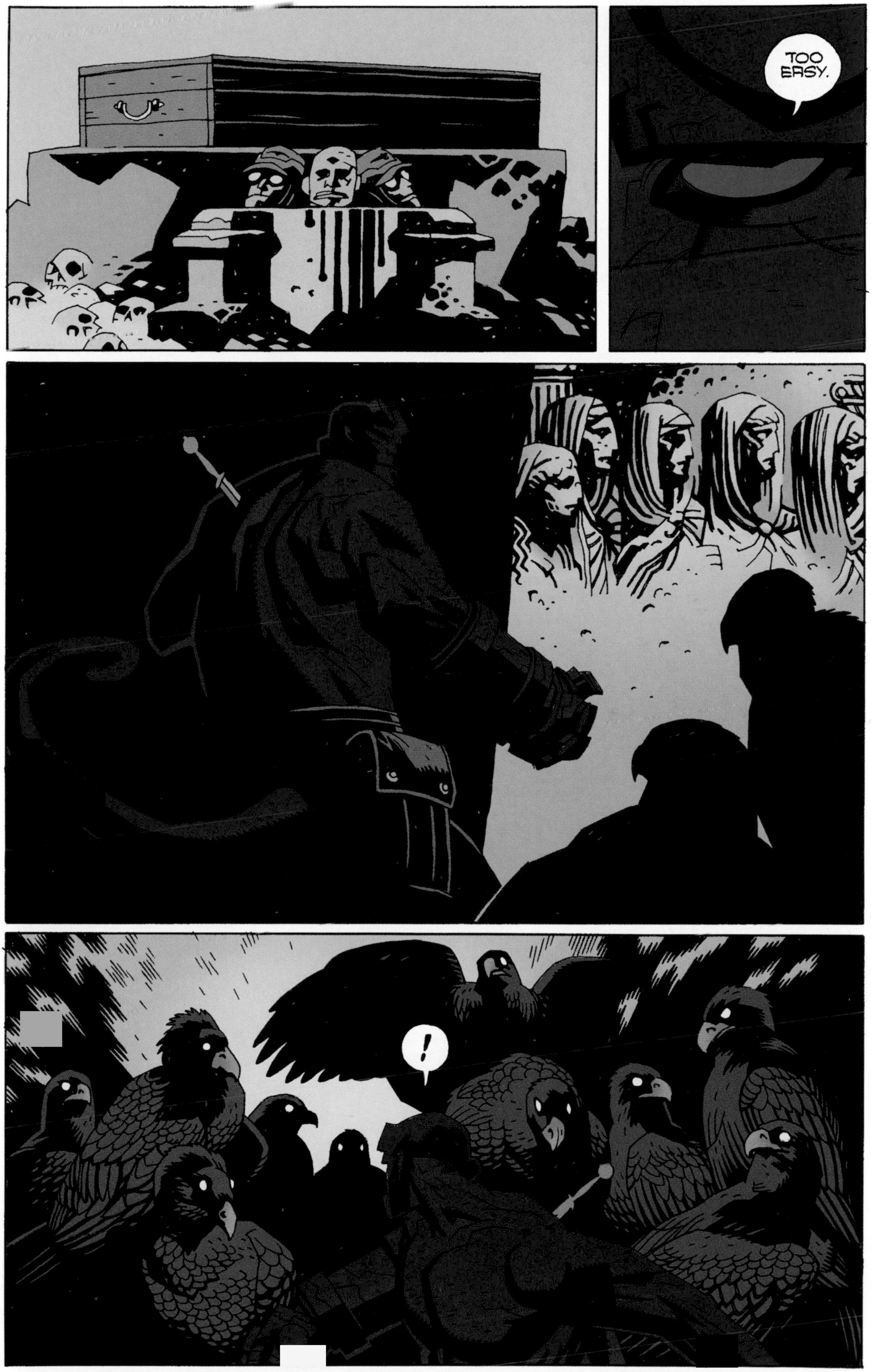
TOO EASY.
!

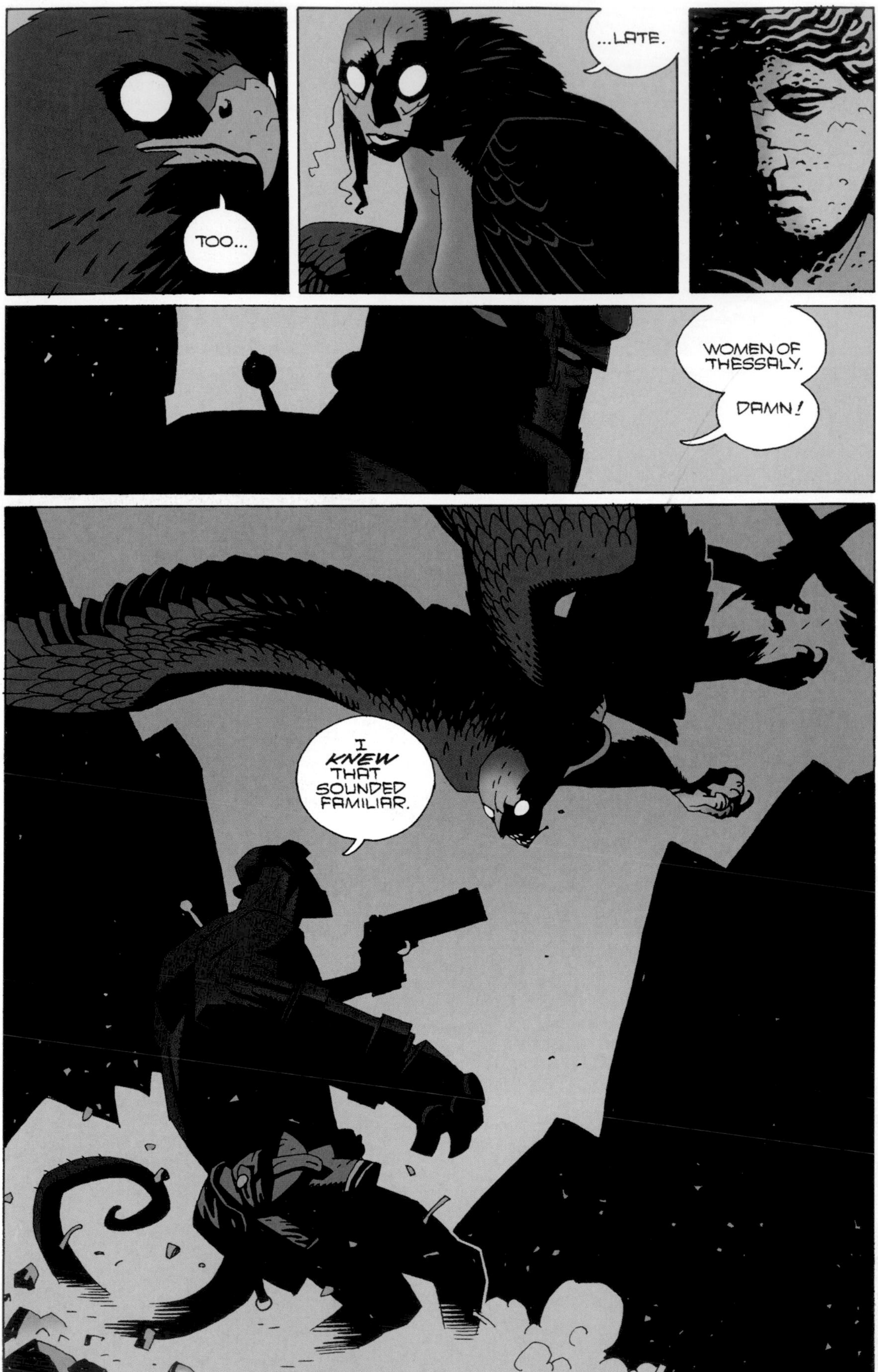
TOO...
...LATE.
WOMEN OF THESSALY.
DAMN!
I KNEW THAT SOUNDED FAMILIAR.

CHAPTER THREE

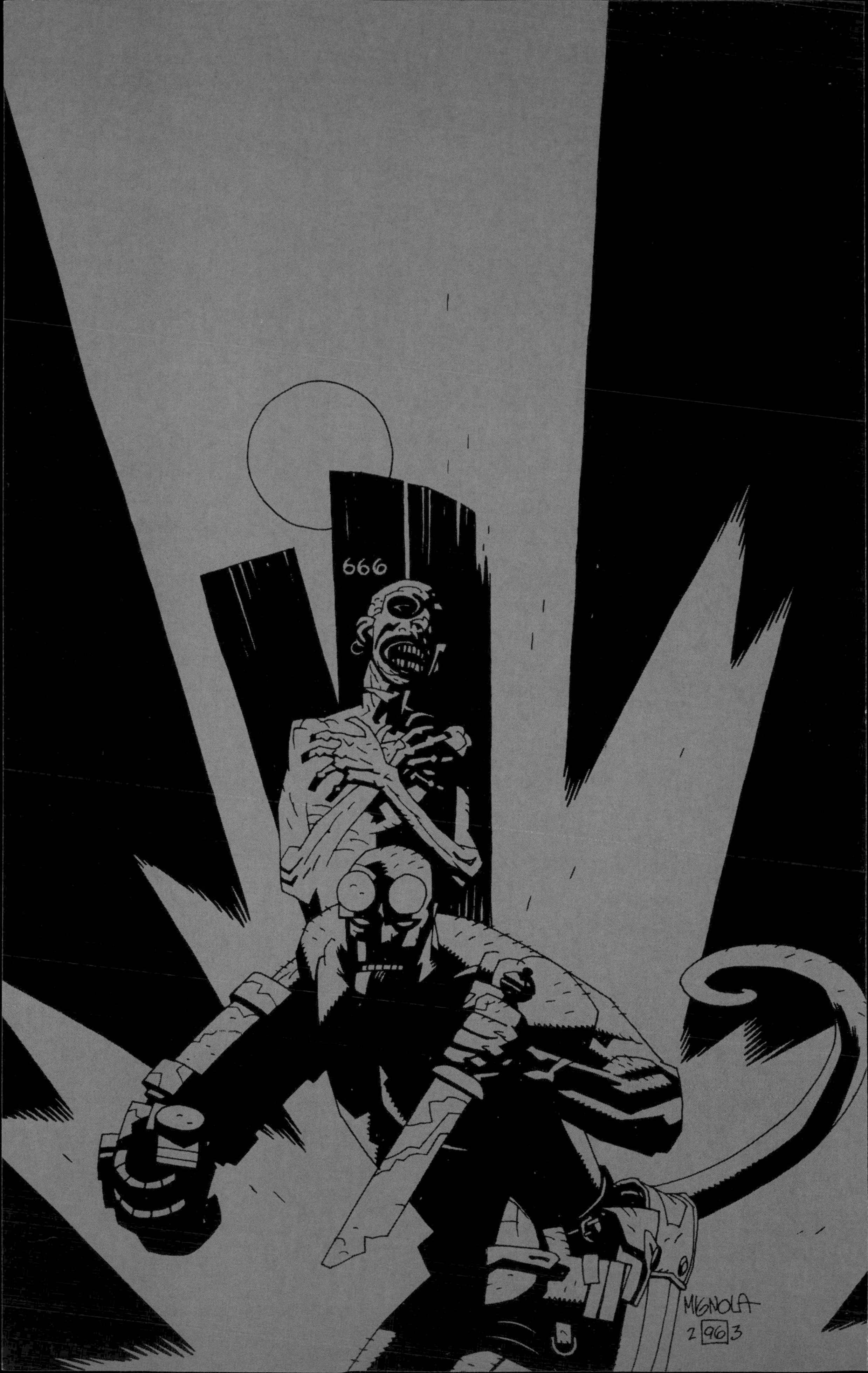
666
MIGNOLA
2 96 3

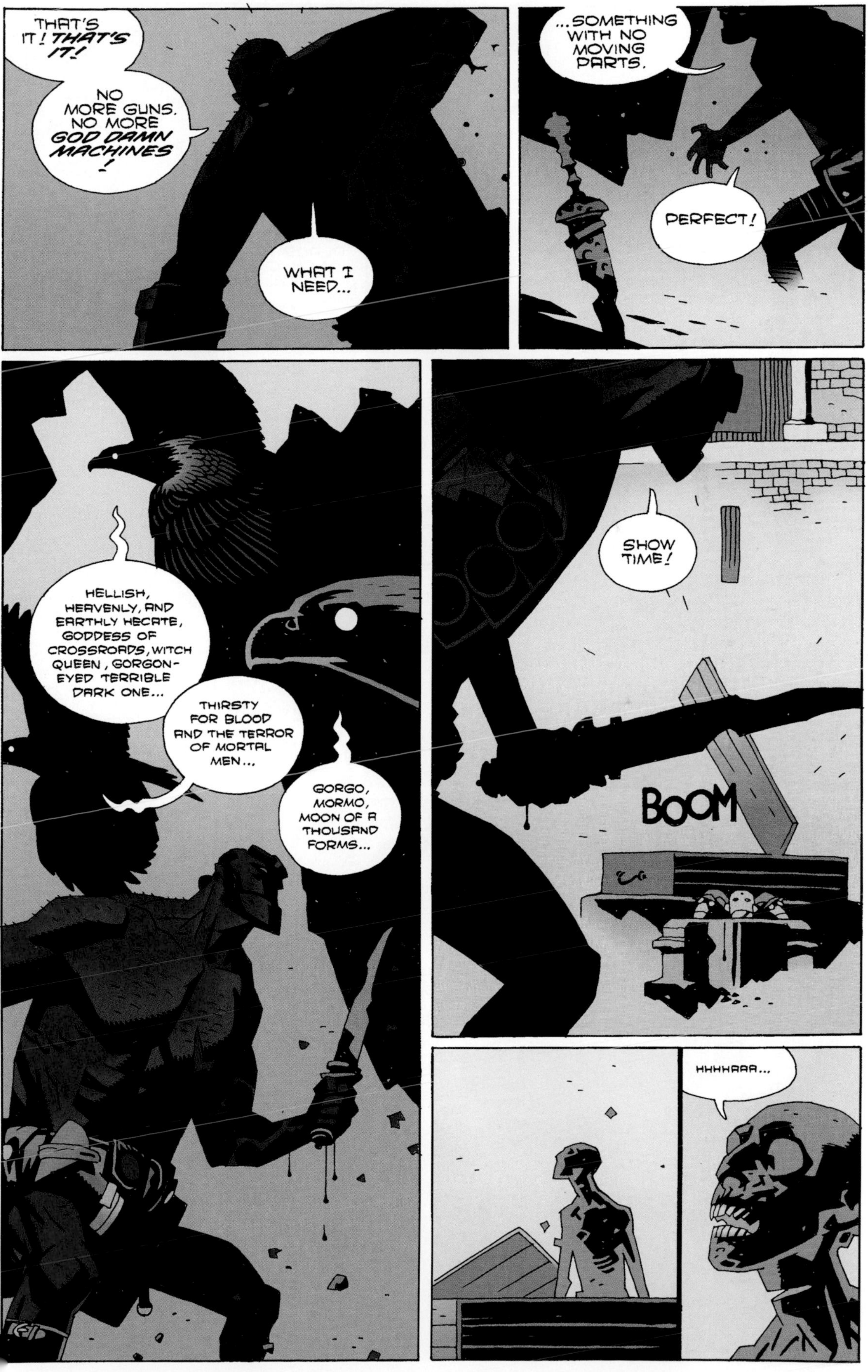
THAT'S IT! THAT'S IT!
NO MORE GUNS. NO MORE GOD DAMN MACHINES!
WHAT I NEED...
...SOMETHING WITH NO MOVING PARTS.
PERFECT!
HELLISH, HEAVENLY, AND EARTHLY HECATE, GODDESS OF CROSSROADS, WITCH QUEEN, GORGON-EYED TERRIBLE DARK ONE...
THIRSTY FOR BLOOD AND THE TERROR OF MORTAL MEN...
GORGO, MORMO, MOON OF A THOUSAND FORMS...
SHOW TIME!
BOOM
HHHHAAA...

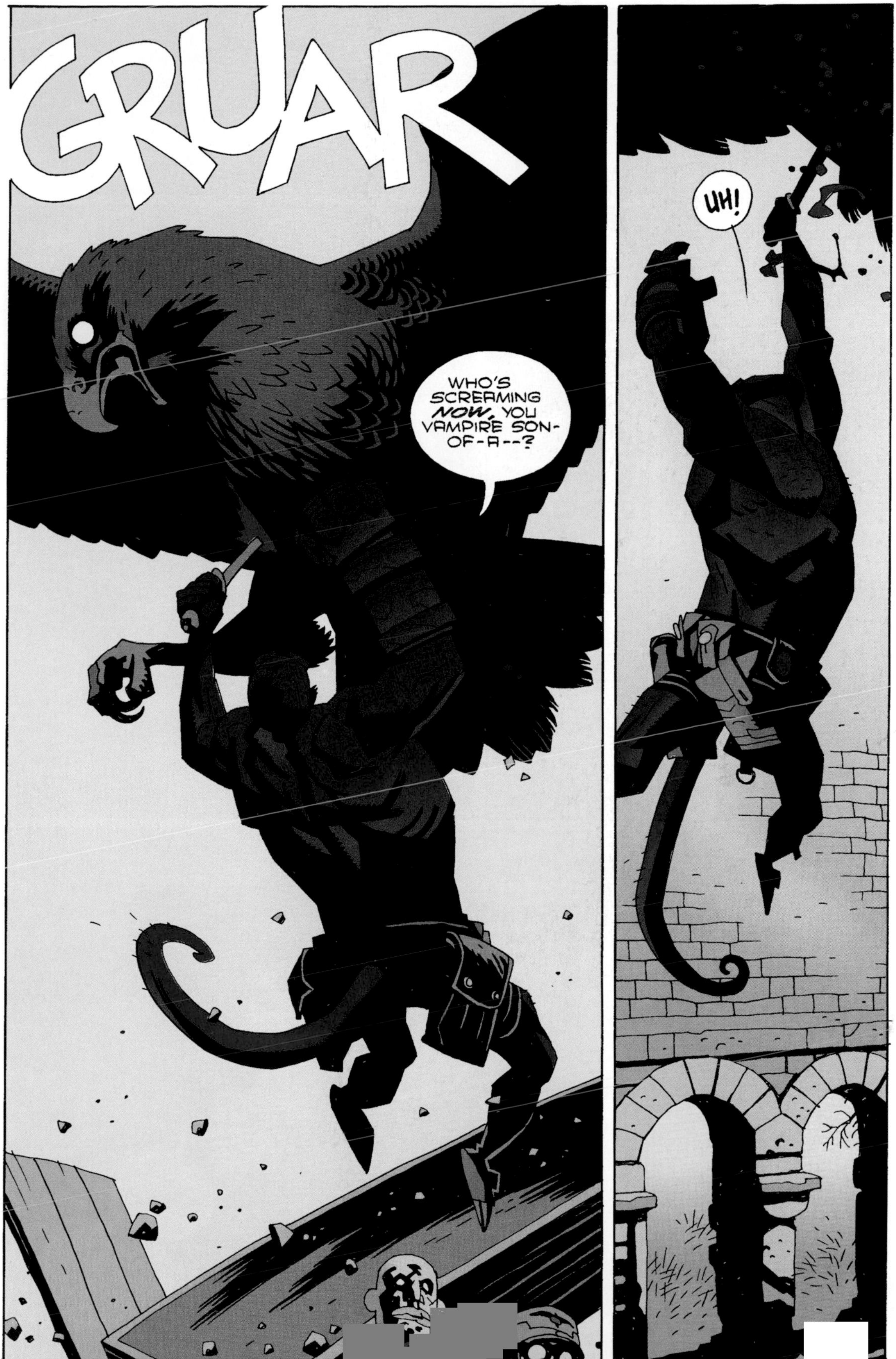
GRUAR
WHO'S SCREAMING NOW, YOU VAMPIRE SON-OF-A--?
UH!

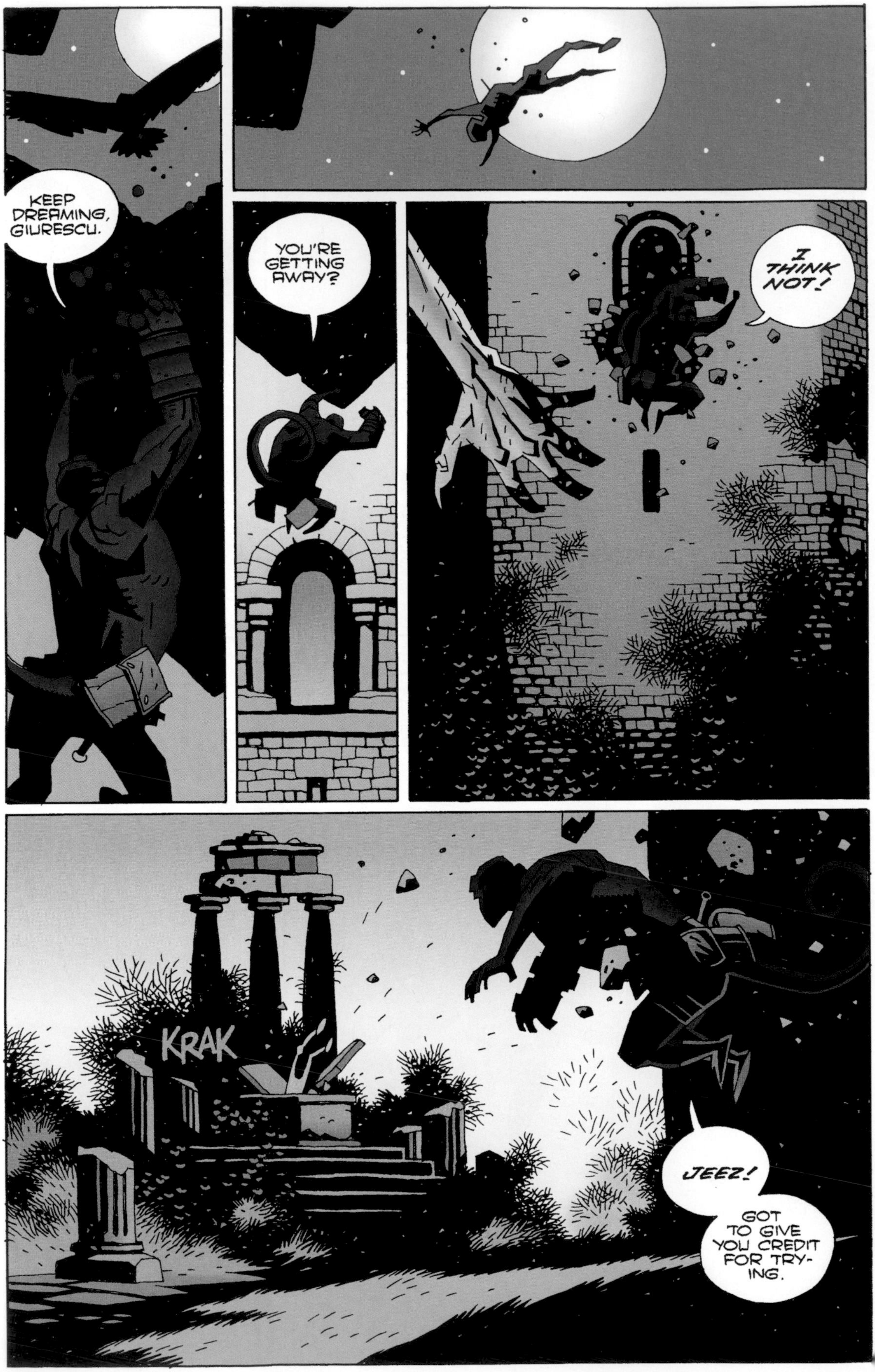
KEEP DREAMING, GIURESCU.
YOU'RE GETTING AWAY?
I THINK NOT!
KRAK
JEEZ!
GOT TO GIVE YOU CREDIT FOR TRY-ING.

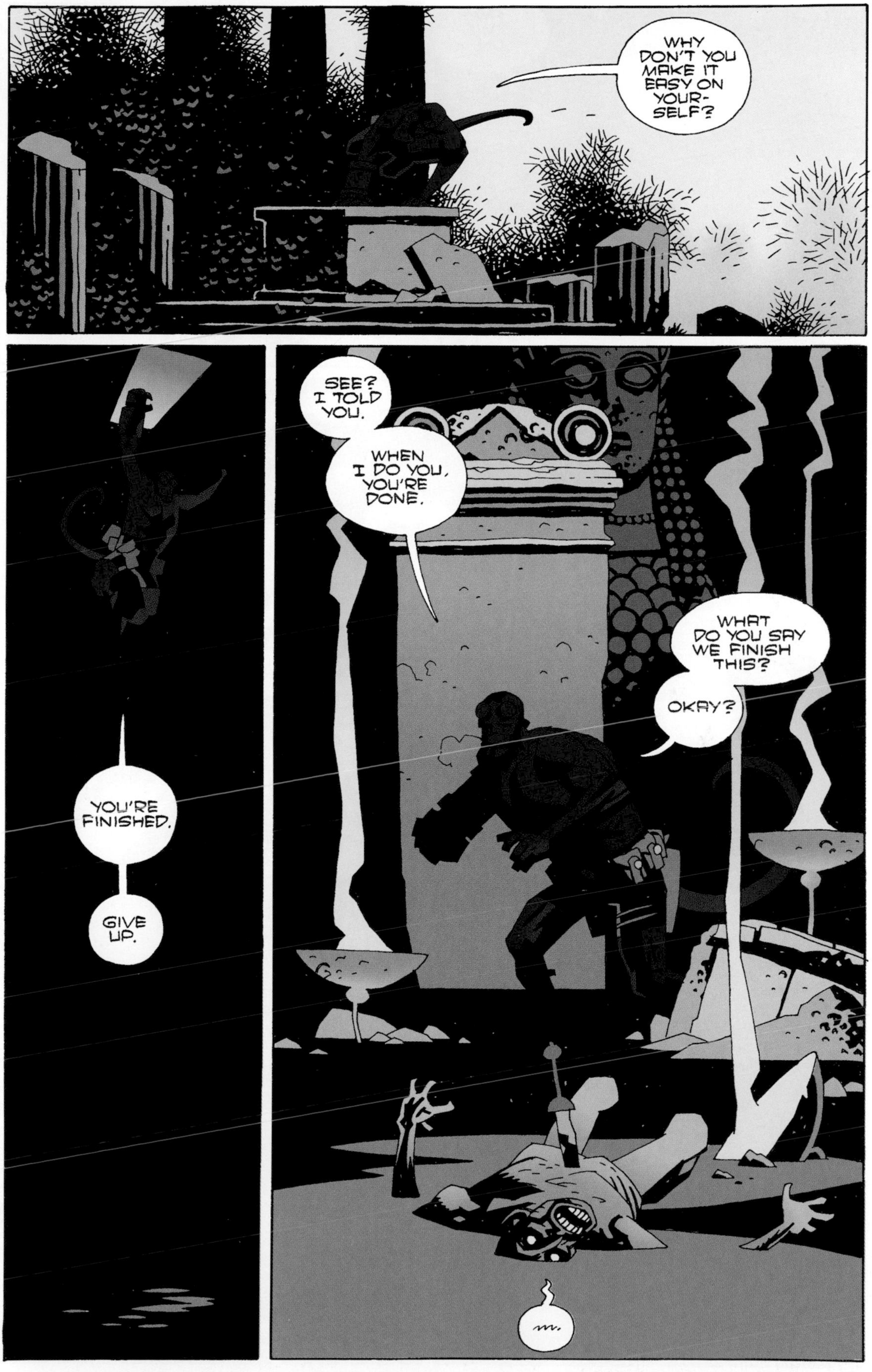
WHY DON'T YOU MAKE IT EASY ON YOUR-SELF?
YOU'RE FINISHED.
GIVE UP.
SEE? I TOLD YOU.
WHEN I DO YOU, YOU'RE DONE.
WHAT DO YOU SAY WE FINISH THIS?
OKAY?

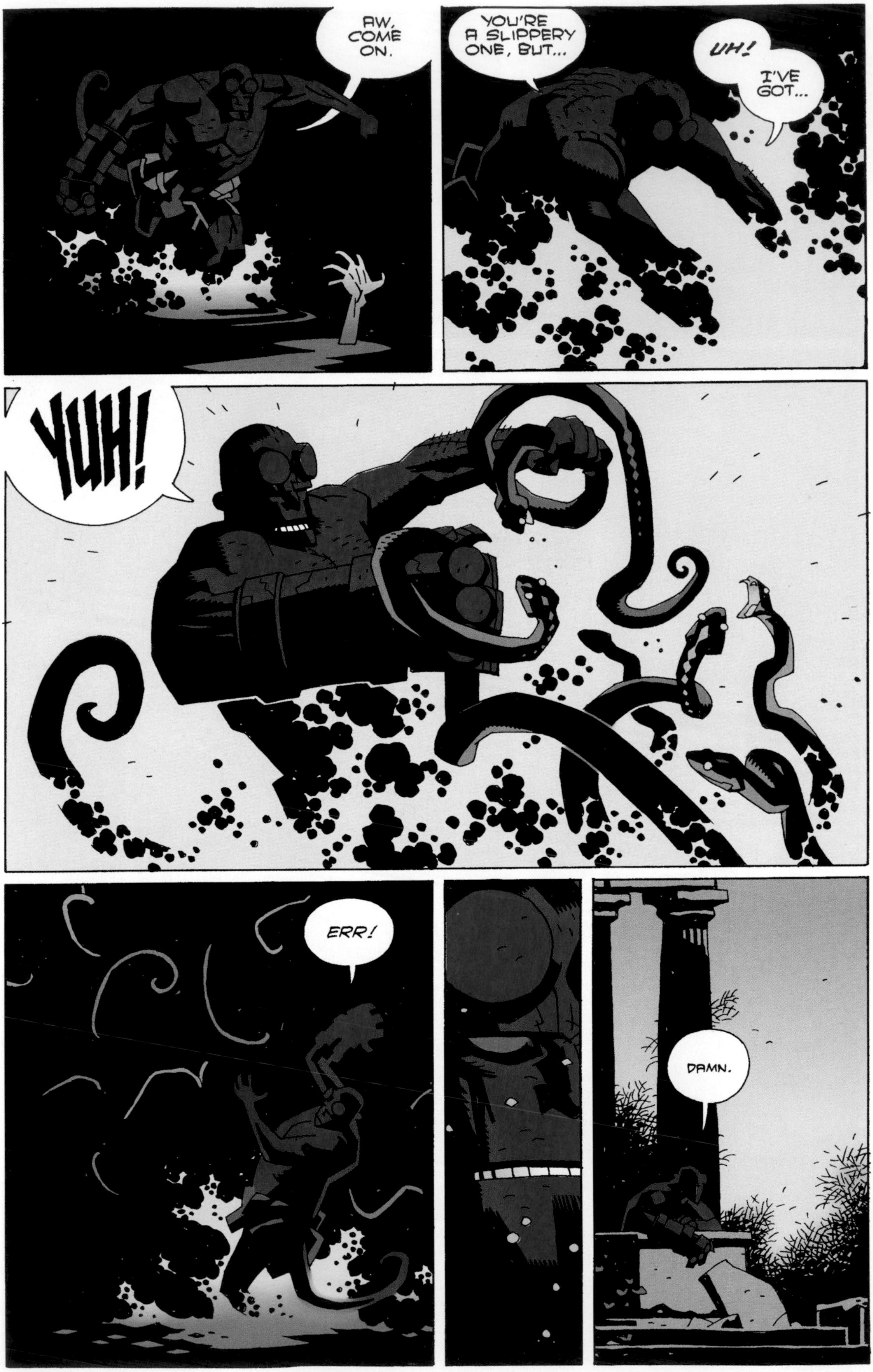
AW, COME ON.
YOU'RE A SLIPPERY ONE, BUT...
UH!
I'VE GOT...
YUH!
ERR!
DAMN.

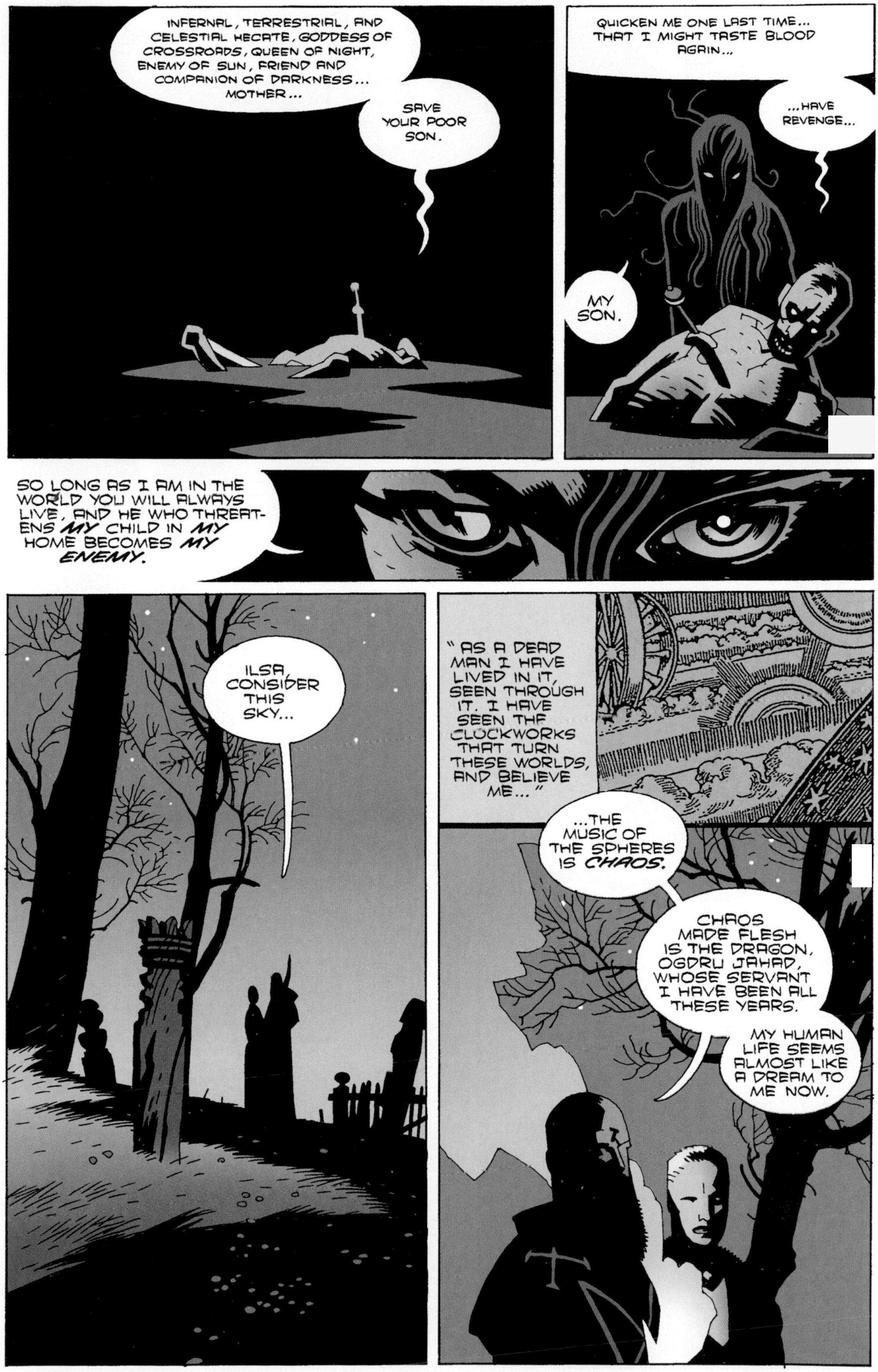

INFERNAL, TERRESTRIAL, AND CELESTIAL HECATE, GODDESS OF CROSSROADS, QUEEN OF NIGHT, ENEMY OF SUN, FRIEND AND COMPANION OF DARKNESS... MOTHER...
SAVE YOUR POOR SON.
QUICKEN ME ONE LAST TIME... THAT I MIGHT TASTE BLOOD AGAIN...
...HAVE REVENGE...
MY SON.
SO LONG AS I AM IN THE WORLD YOU WILL ALWAYS LIVE, AND HE WHO THREATENS MY CHILD IN MY HOME BECOMES MY ENEMY.
ILSA, CONSIDER THIS SKY...
"AS A DEAD MAN I HAVE LIVED IN IT, SEEN THROUGH IT. I HAVE SEEN THE CLOCKWORKS THAT TURN THESE WORLDS, AND BELIEVE ME..."
...THE MUSIC OF THE SPHERES IS CHAOS.
CHAOS MADE FLESH IS THE DRAGON, OGDRU JAHAD, WHOSE SERVANT I HAVE BEEN ALL THESE YEARS.
MY HUMAN LIFE SEEMS ALMOST LIKE A DREAM TO ME NOW.

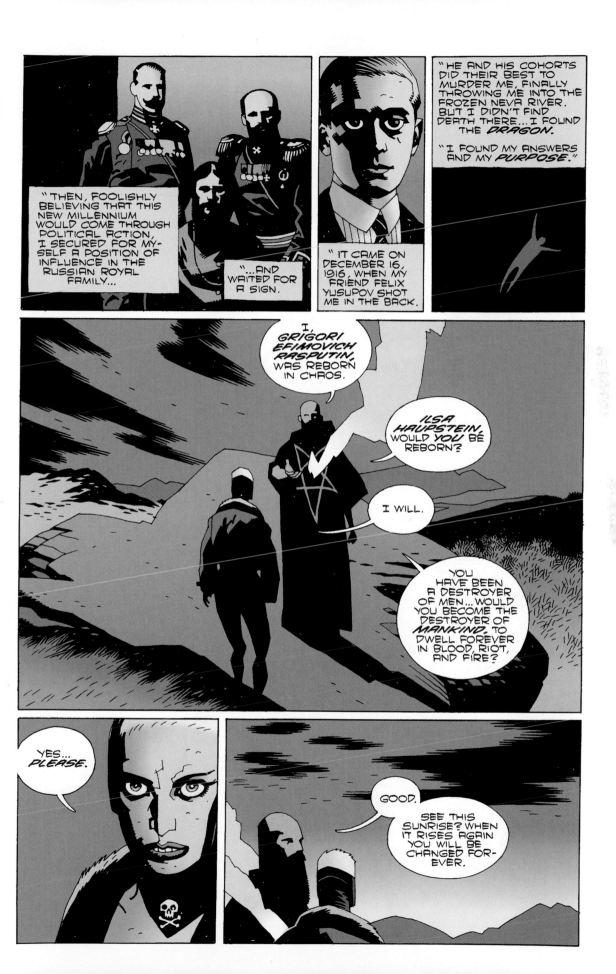

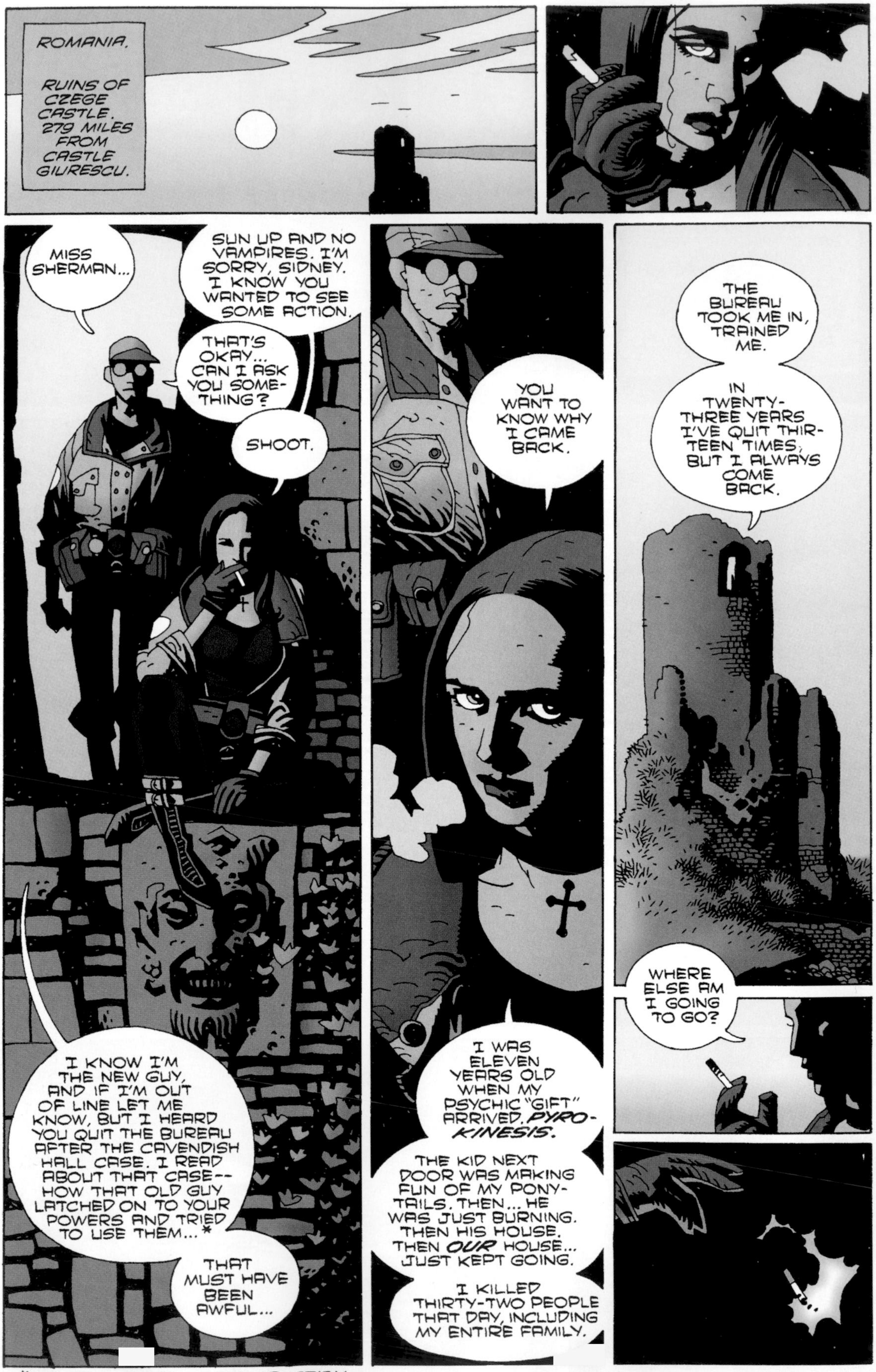

ROMANIA.
RUINS OF CZEGE CASTLE. 279 MILES FROM CASTLE GIURESCU.
MISS SHERMAN...
SUN UP AND NO VAMPIRES. I'M SORRY, SIDNEY. I KNOW YOU WANTED TO SEE SOME ACTION.
THAT'S OKAY... CAN I ASK YOU SOME-THING?
SHOOT.
I KNOW I'M THE NEW GUY, AND IF I'M OUT OF LINE LET ME KNOW, BUT I HEARD YOU QUIT THE BUREAU AFTER THE CAVENDISH HALL CASE. I READ ABOUT THAT CASE-- HOW THAT OLD GUY LATCHED ON TO YOUR POWERS AND TRIED TO USE THEM...*
THAT MUST HAVE BEEN AWFUL...
YOU WANT TO KNOW WHY I CAME BACK.
I WAS ELEVEN YEARS OLD WHEN MY PSYCHIC "GIFT" ARRIVED. PYRO-KINESIS.
THE KID NEXT DOOR WAS MAKING FUN OF MY PONY-TAILS. THEN... HE WAS JUST BURNING. THEN HIS HOUSE. THEN OUR HOUSE... JUST KEPT GOING.
I KILLED THIRTY-TWO PEOPLE THAT DAY, INCLUDING MY ENTIRE FAMILY.
THE BUREAU TOOK ME IN, TRAINED ME.
IN TWENTY-THREE YEARS I'VE QUIT THIR-TEEN TIMES, BUT I ALWAYS COME BACK.
WHERE ELSE AM I GOING TO GO?

*HELLBOY: SEED OF DESTRUCTION

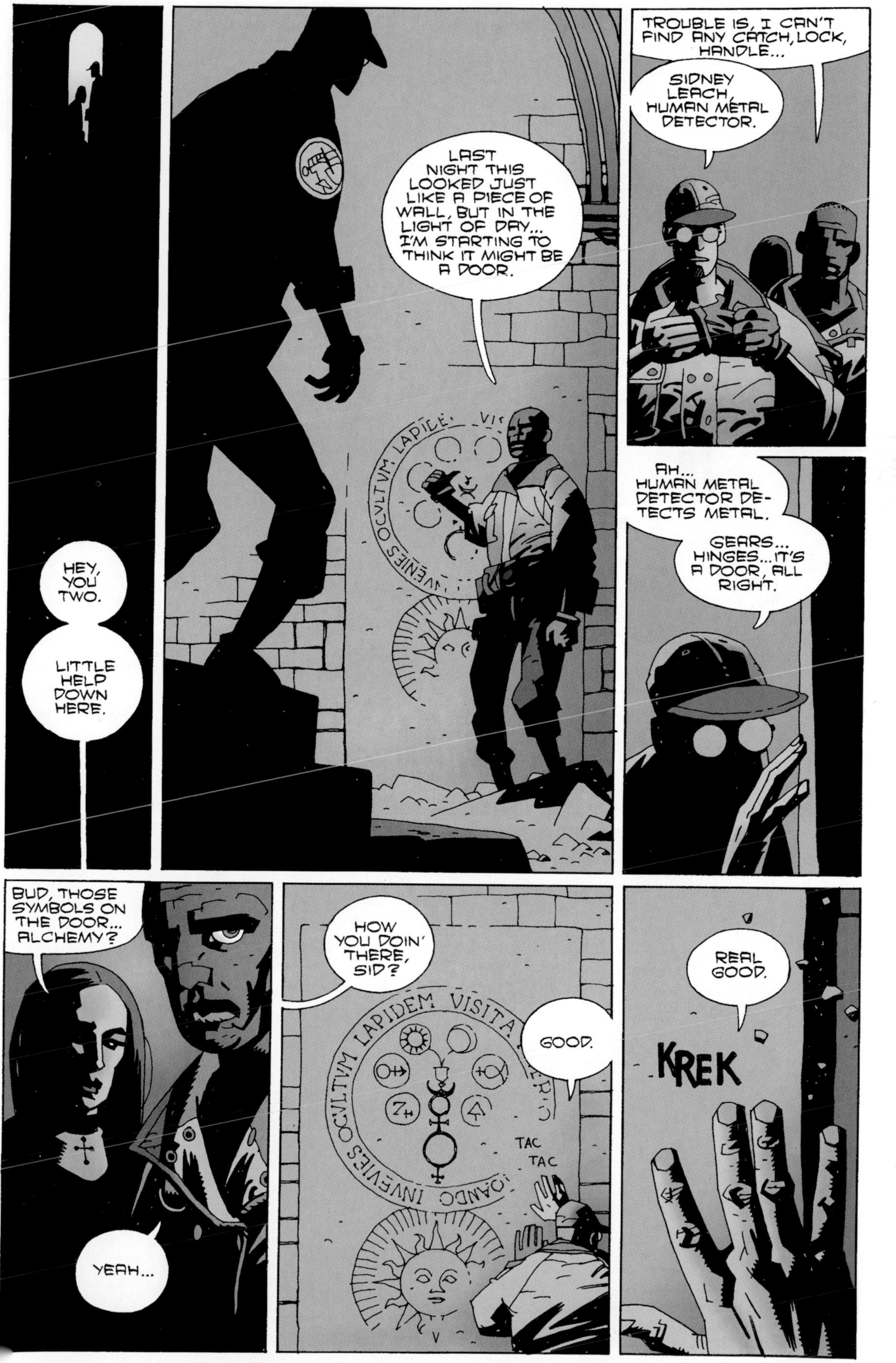
LAST NIGHT THIS LOOKED JUST LIKE A PIECE OF WALL, BUT IN THE LIGHT OF DAY... I'M STARTING TO THINK IT MIGHT BE A DOOR.
HEY, YOU TWO.
LITTLE HELP DOWN HERE.
TROUBLE IS, I CAN'T FIND ANY CATCH, LOCK, HANDLE...
SIDNEY LEACH, HUMAN METAL DETECTOR.
AH... HUMAN METAL DETECTOR DETECTS METAL.
GEARS... HINGES... IT'S A DOOR, ALL RIGHT.
BUD, THOSE SYMBOLS ON THE DOOR... ALCHEMY?
YEAH...
HOW YOU DOIN' THERE, SID?
VISITA INTERIORA TERRAE RECTIFICANDO INVENIES OCCULTUM LAPIDEM
GOOD.
TAC
TAC
REAL GOOD.
KREK

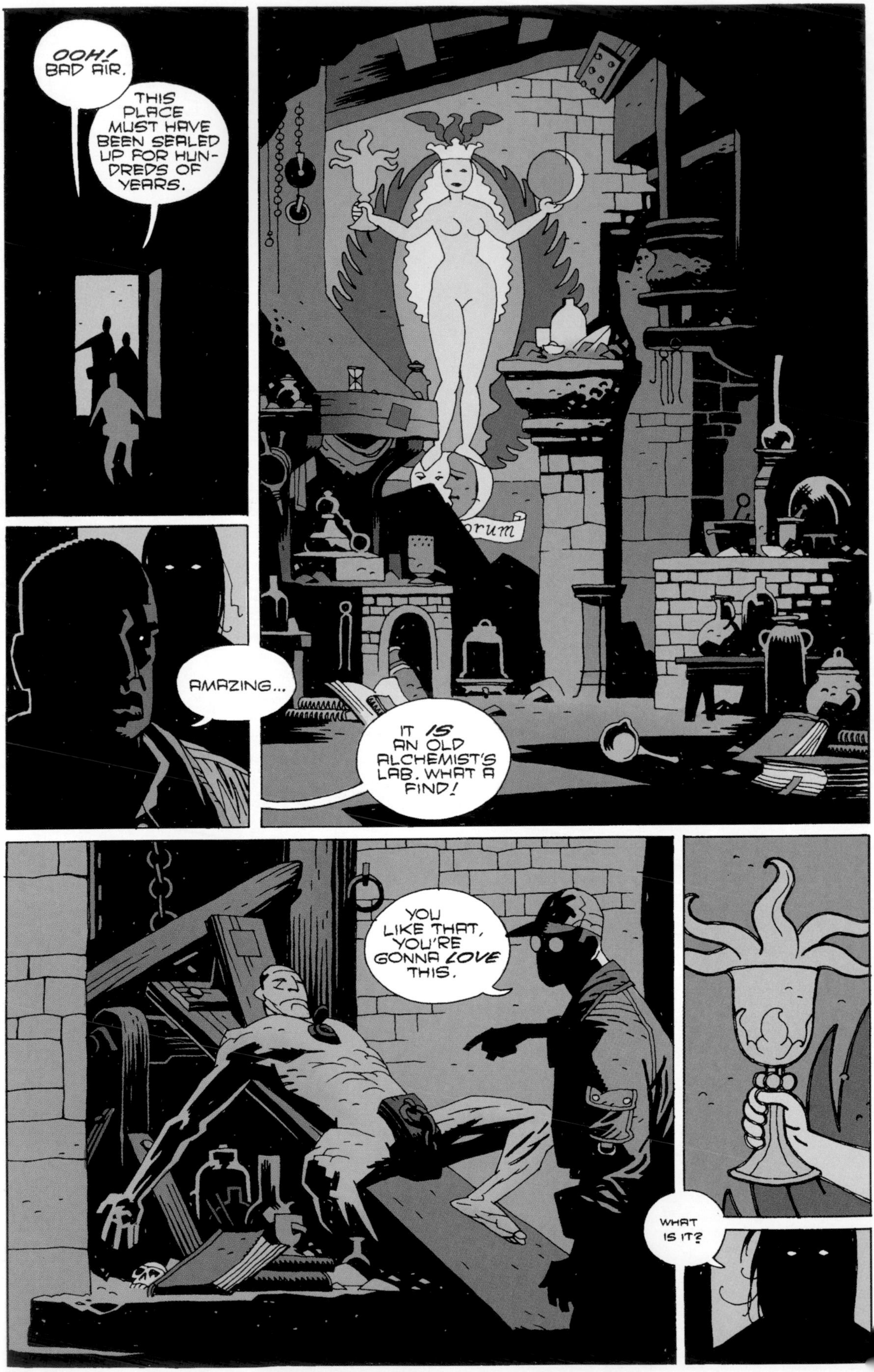
OOH! BAD AIR.
THIS PLACE MUST HAVE BEEN SEALED UP FOR HUN-DREDS OF YEARS.
AMAZING...
...rum
IT IS AN OLD ALCHEMIST'S LAB. WHAT A FIND!
YOU LIKE THAT, YOU'RE GONNA LOVE THIS.
WHAT IS IT?

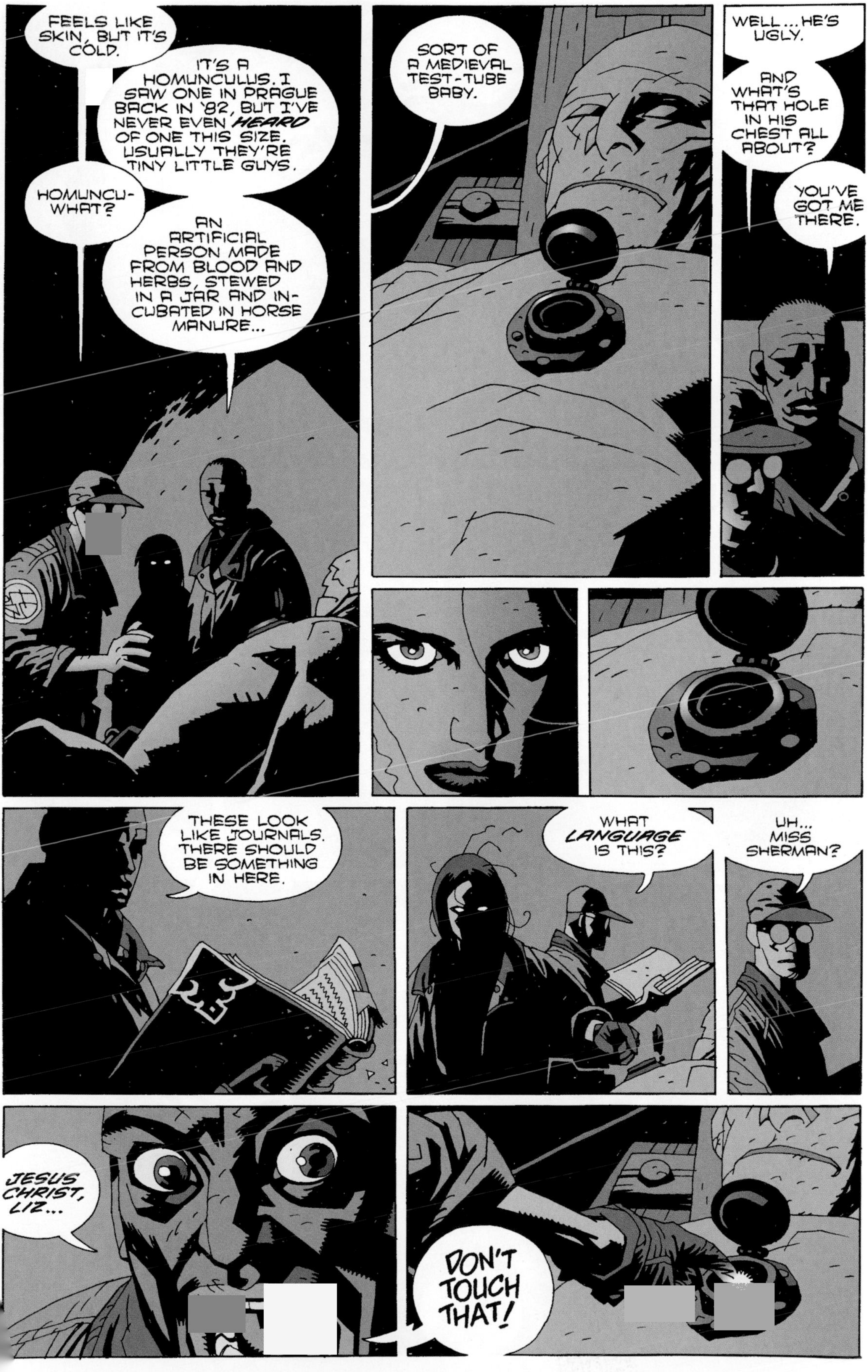
FEELS LIKE SKIN, BUT IT'S COLD.
IT'S A HOMUNCULUS. I SAW ONE IN PRAGUE BACK IN '82, BUT I'VE NEVER EVEN *HEARD* OF ONE THIS SIZE. USUALLY THEY'RE TINY LITTLE GUYS.
HOMUNCU-WHAT?
AN ARTIFICIAL PERSON MADE FROM BLOOD AND HERBS, STEWED IN A JAR AND IN-CUBATED IN HORSE MANURE...
SORT OF A MEDIEVAL TEST-TUBE BABY.
WELL... HE'S UGLY.
AND WHAT'S THAT HOLE IN HIS CHEST ALL ABOUT?
YOU'VE GOT ME THERE.
THESE LOOK LIKE JOURNALS. THERE SHOULD BE SOMETHING IN HERE.
WHAT *LANGUAGE* IS THIS?
UH... MISS SHERMAN?
JESUS CHRIST, LIZ...
DON'T TOUCH THAT!

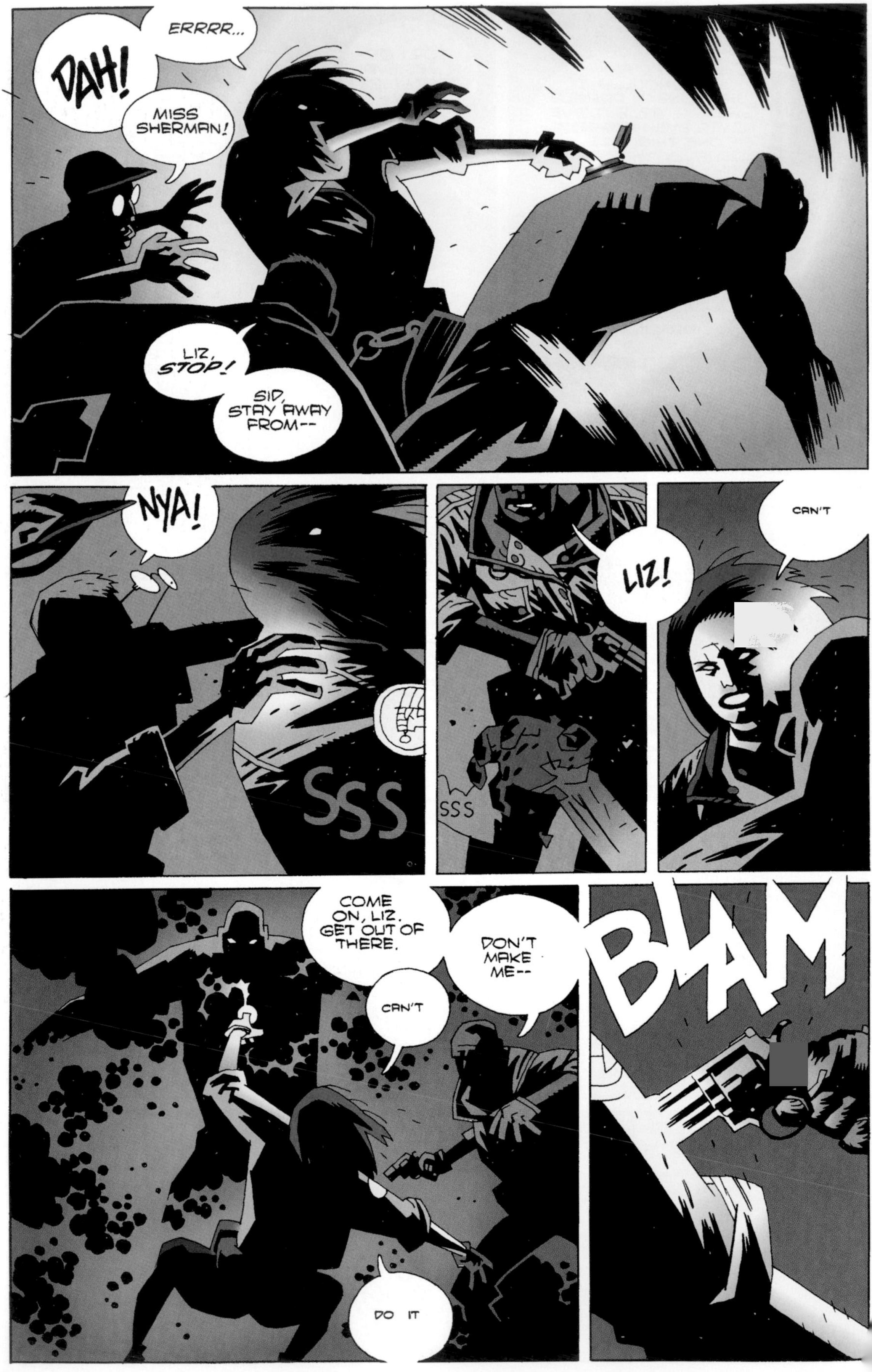

DAH!
ERRRR...
MISS SHERMAN!
LIZ, STOP!
SID, STAY AWAY FROM--
NYA!
SSS
SSS
LIZ!
CAN'T
COME ON, LIZ. GET OUT OF THERE.
DON'T MAKE ME--
CAN'T
DO IT
BLAM

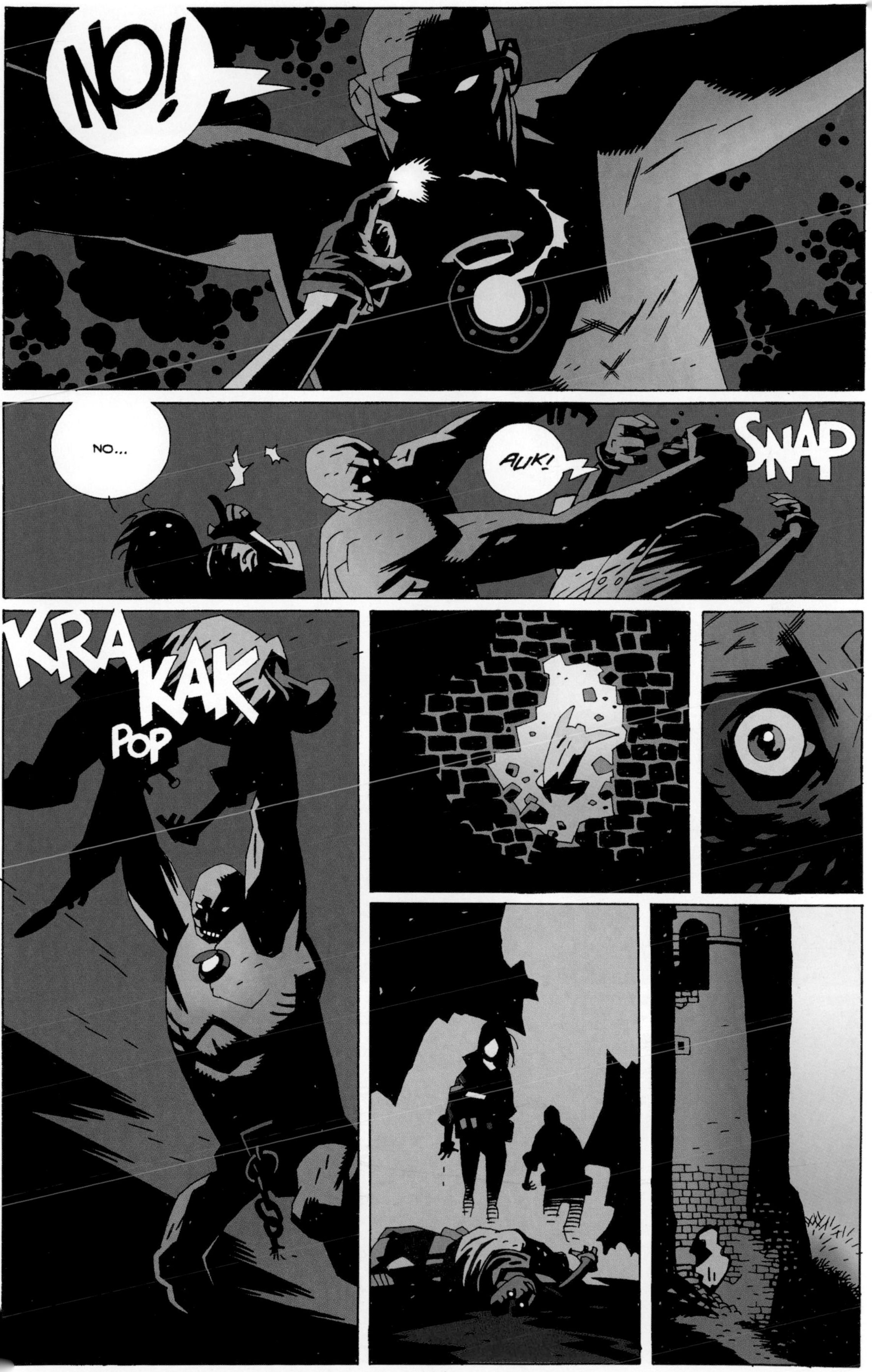
NO!
NO...
AUK!
SNAP
KRA
KAK
POP

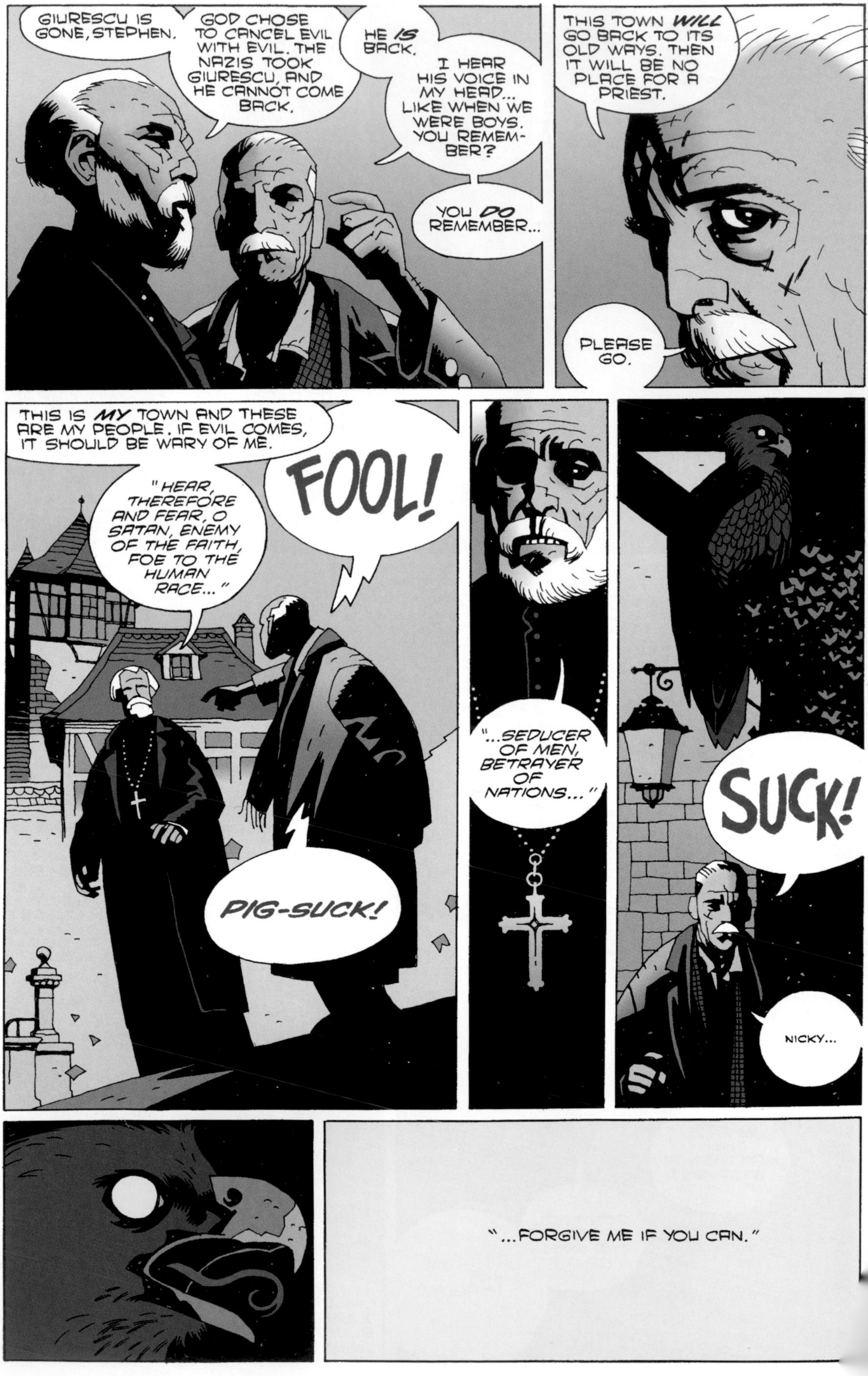
GIURESCU IS GONE, STEPHEN.
GOD CHOSE TO CANCEL EVIL WITH EVIL. THE NAZIS TOOK GIURESCU, AND HE CANNOT COME BACK.
HE IS BACK.
I HEAR HIS VOICE IN MY HEAD... LIKE WHEN WE WERE BOYS. YOU REMEMBER?
YOU DO REMEMBER...
THIS TOWN WILL GO BACK TO ITS OLD WAYS. THEN IT WILL BE NO PLACE FOR A PRIEST.
PLEASE GO.
THIS IS MY TOWN AND THESE ARE MY PEOPLE. IF EVIL COMES, IT SHOULD BE WARY OF ME.
"HEAR, THEREFORE AND FEAR, O SATAN, ENEMY OF THE FAITH, FOE TO THE HUMAN RACE..."
FOOL!
PIG-SUCK!
"...SEDUCER OF MEN, BETRAYER OF NATIONS..."
SUCK!
NICKY...
"...FORGIVE ME IF YOU CAN."

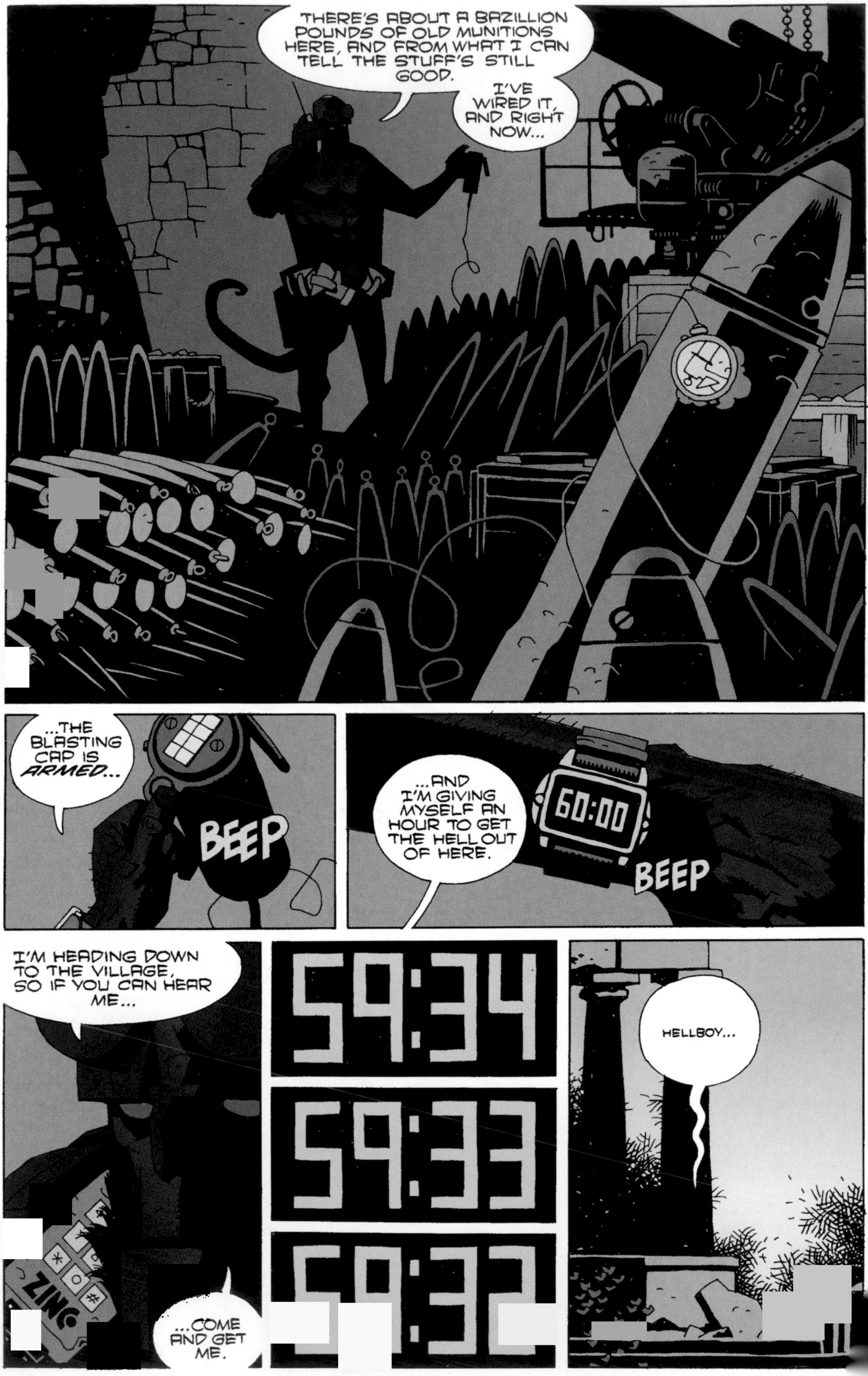
THERE'S ABOUT A BAZILLION POUNDS OF OLD MUNITIONS HERE, AND FROM WHAT I CAN TELL THE STUFF'S STILL GOOD.
I'VE WIRED IT, AND RIGHT NOW...
...THE BLASTING CAP IS *ARMED...*
BEEP
...AND I'M GIVING MYSELF AN HOUR TO GET THE HELL OUT OF HERE.
60:00
BEEP
I'M HEADING DOWN TO THE VILLAGE, SO IF YOU CAN HEAR ME...
ZING
...COME AND GET ME.
59:34
59:33
59:32
HELLBOY...

CHAPTER FOUR

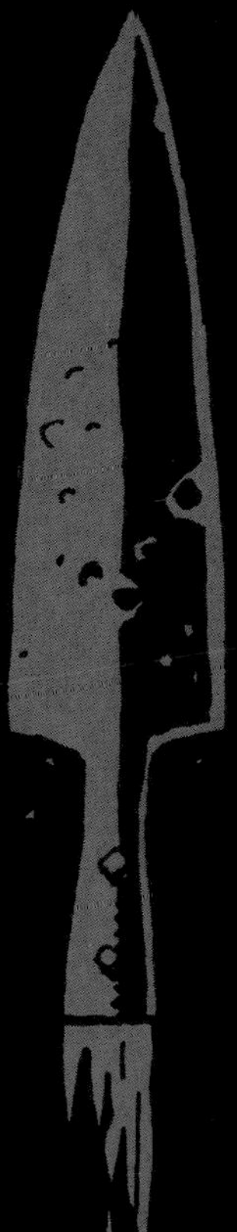

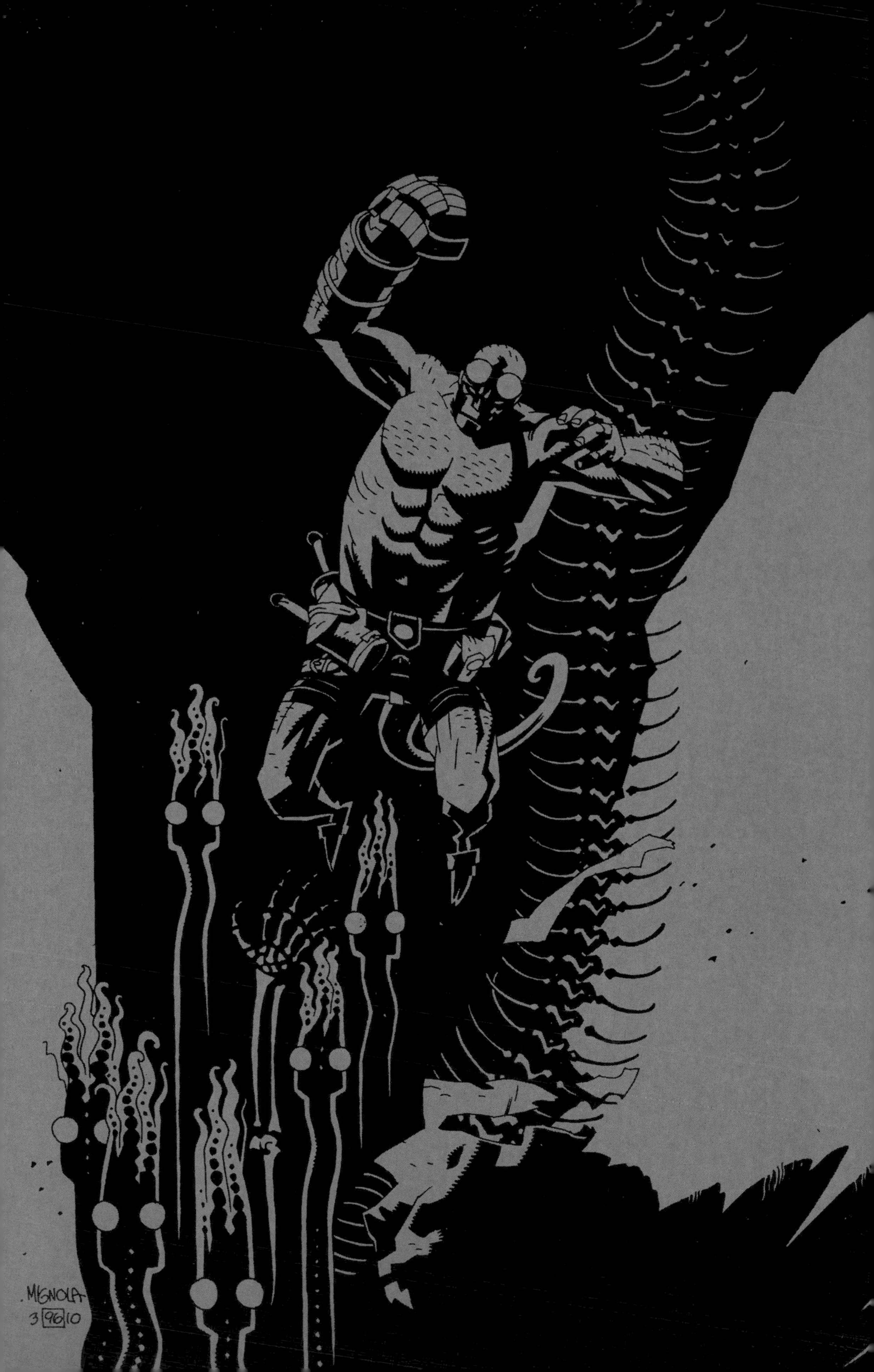
MIGNOLA
3 96 10

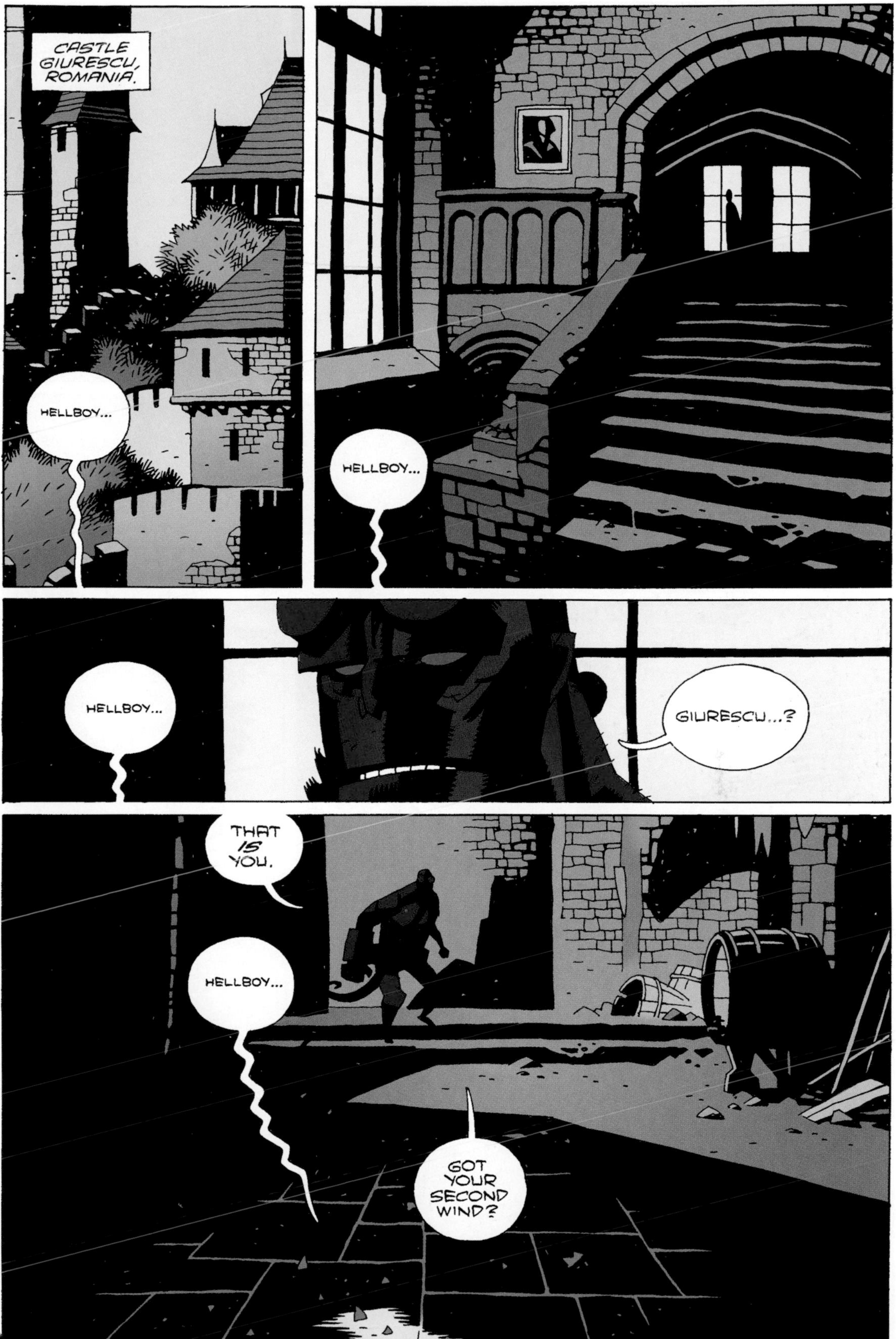
CASTLE GIURESCU, ROMANIA.
HELLBOY...
HELLBOY...
HELLBOY...
GIURESCU...?
THAT IS YOU.
HELLBOY...
GOT YOUR SECOND WIND?

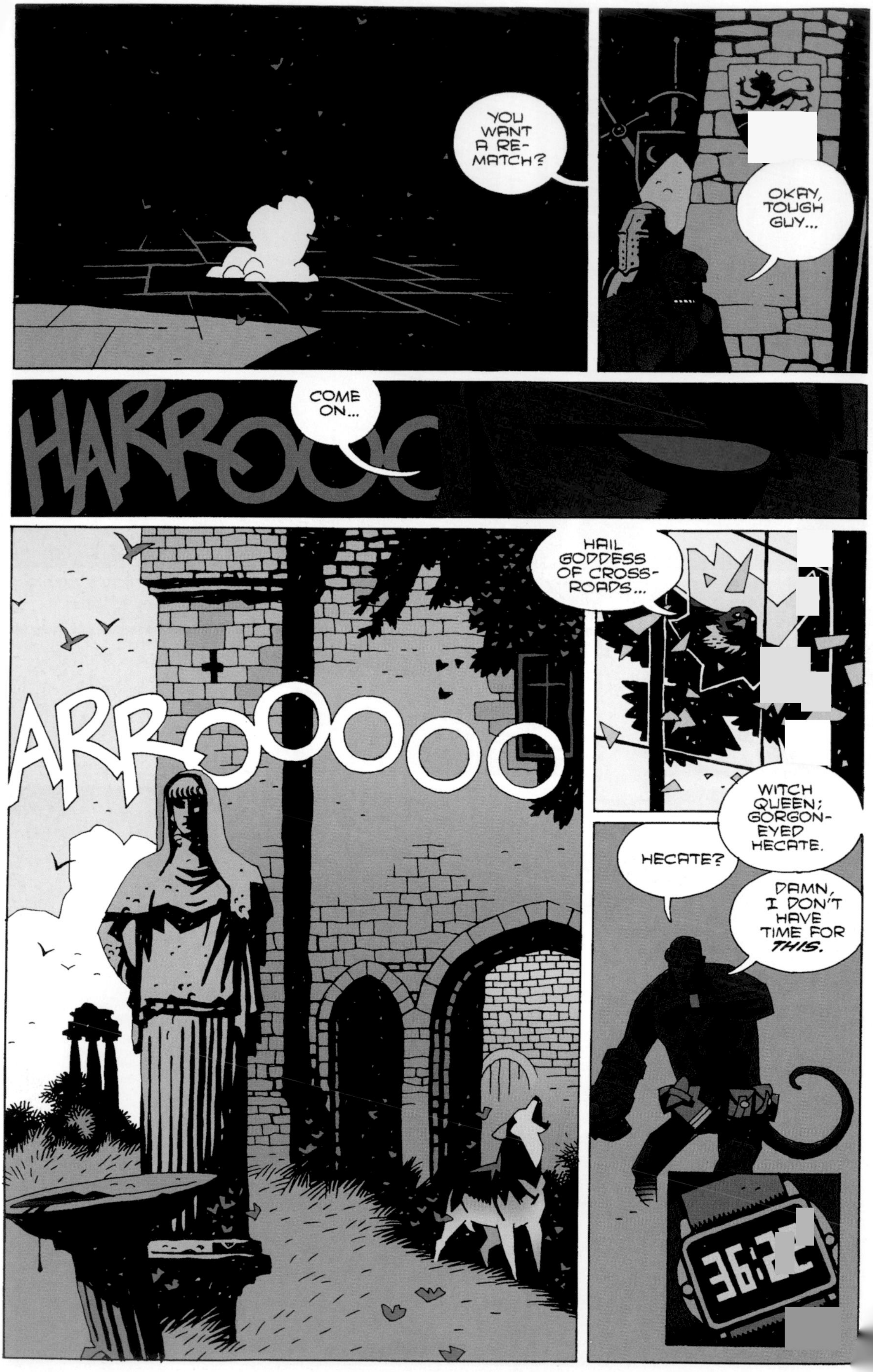
YOU WANT A RE-MATCH?
OKAY, TOUGH GUY...
HARROOO
COME ON...
ARROOOOOO
HAIL GODDESS OF CROSS-ROADS...
WITCH QUEEN; GORGON-EYED HECATE.
HECATE?
DAMN, I DON'T HAVE TIME FOR *THIS.*

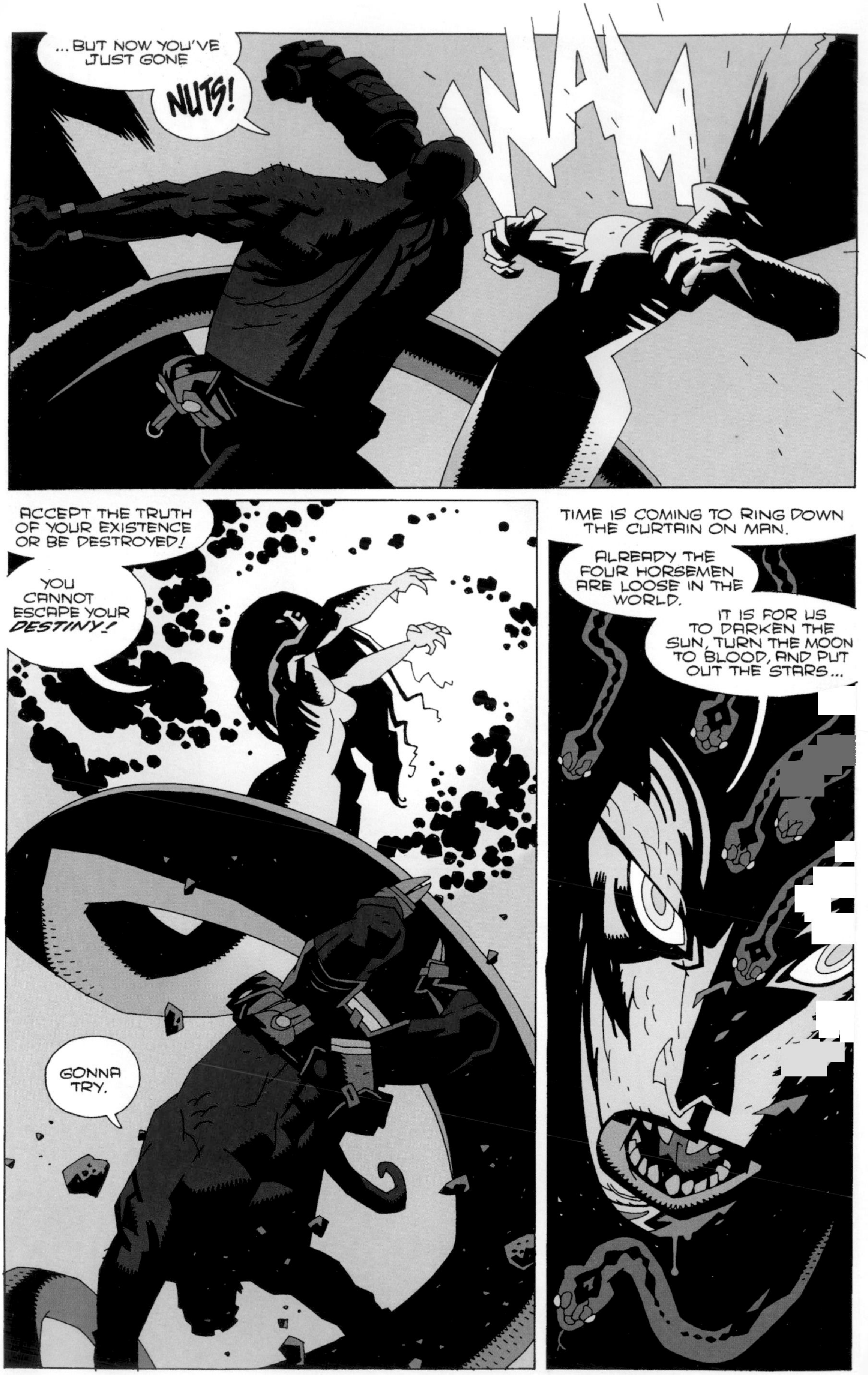

...BUT NOW YOU'VE JUST GONE NUTS!
WAM
ACCEPT THE TRUTH OF YOUR EXISTENCE OR BE DESTROYED!
YOU CANNOT ESCAPE YOUR DESTINY!
GONNA TRY.
TIME IS COMING TO RING DOWN THE CURTAIN ON MAN.
ALREADY THE FOUR HORSEMEN ARE LOOSE IN THE WORLD.
IT IS FOR US TO DARKEN THE SUN, TURN THE MOON TO BLOOD, AND PUT OUT THE STARS...

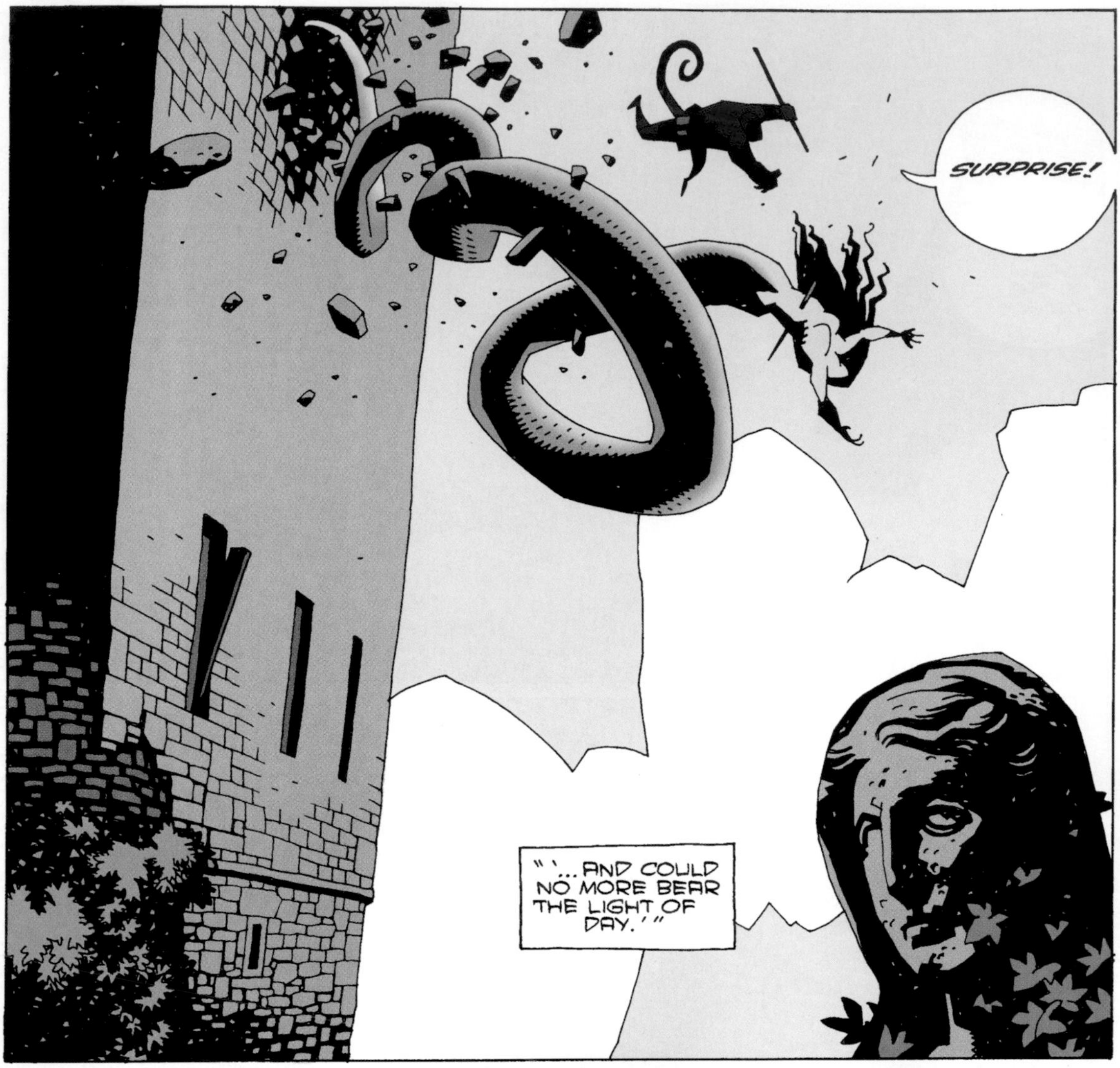
SURPRISE!
"'...AND COULD NO MORE BEAR THE LIGHT OF DAY.'"

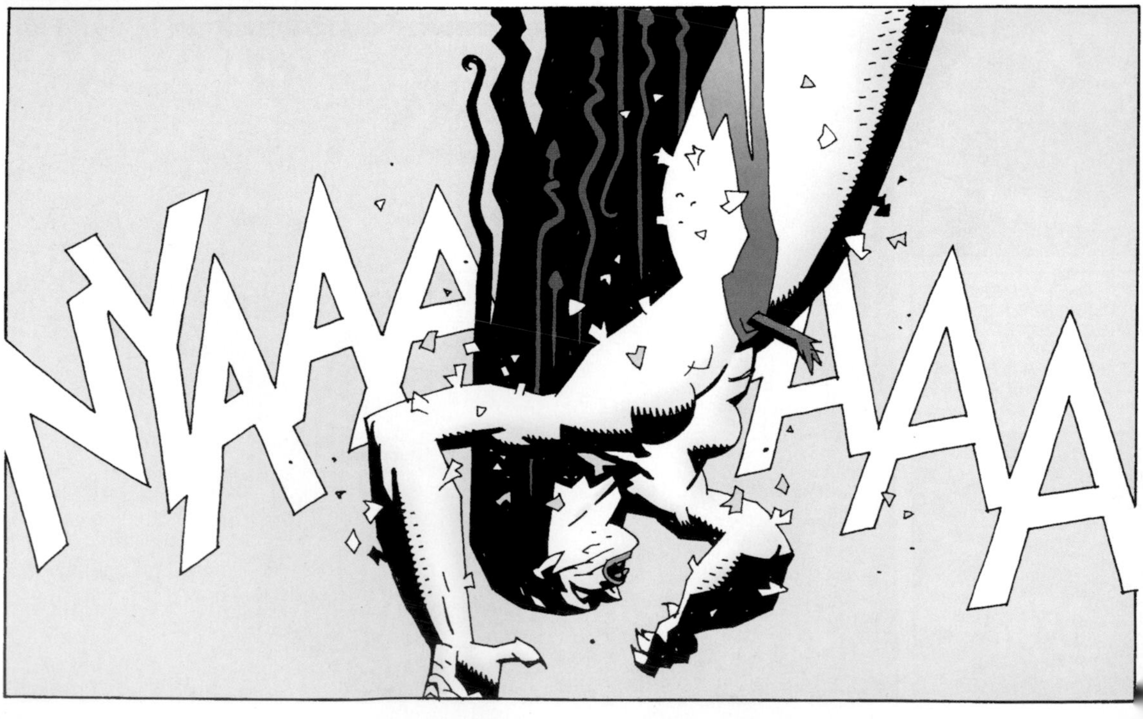
NYAAAHAAA

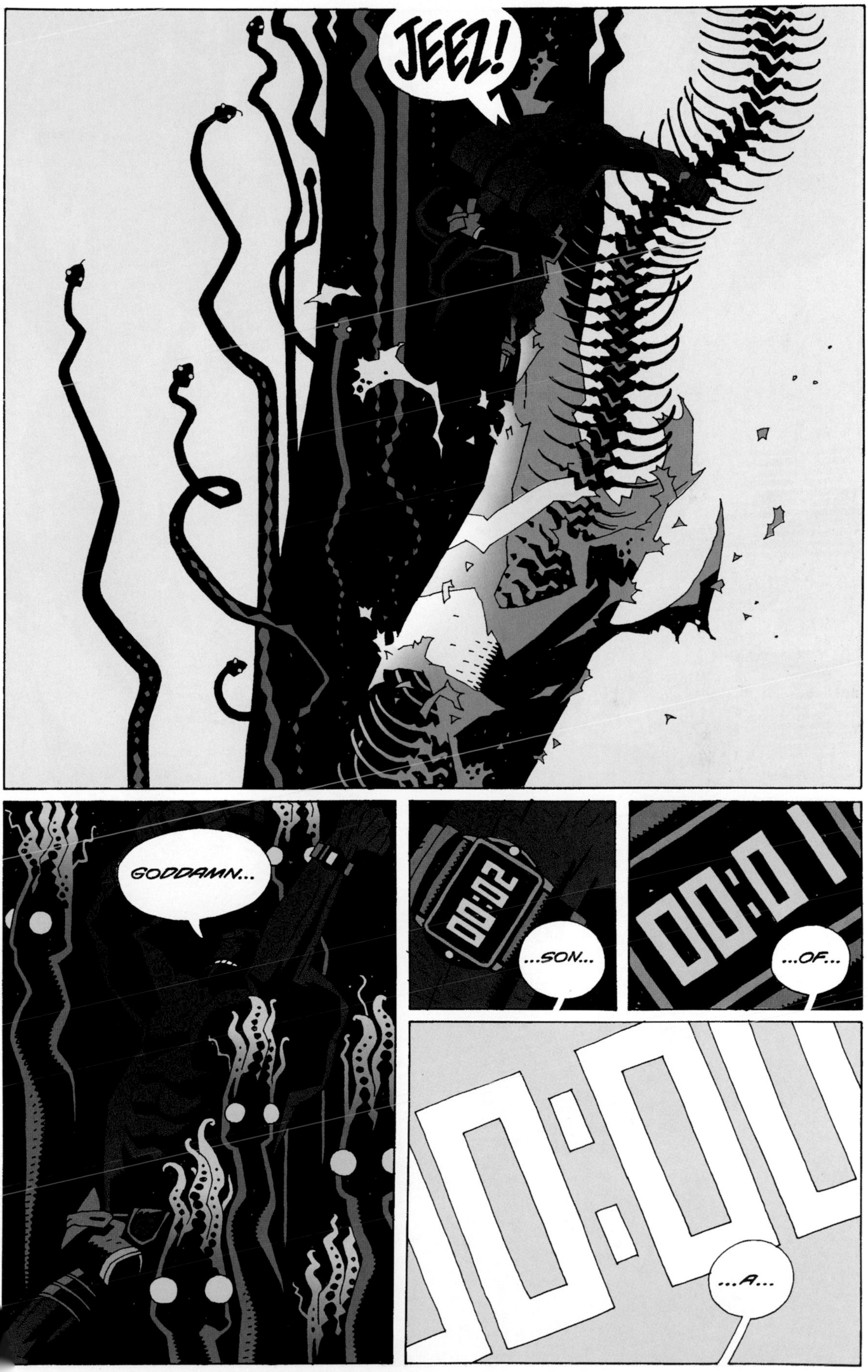
JEEZ!
GODDAMN...
...SON...
...OF...
...A...

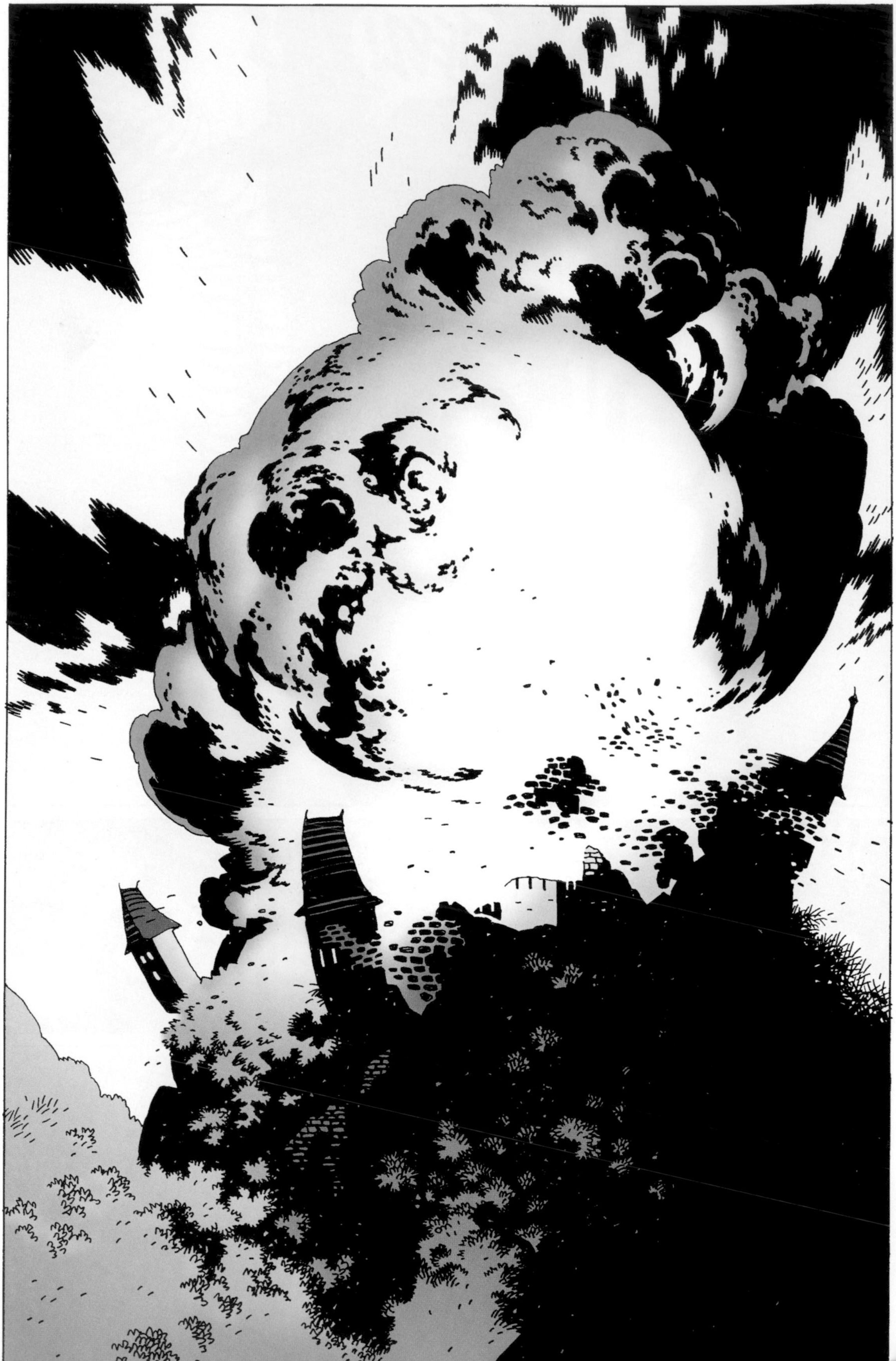

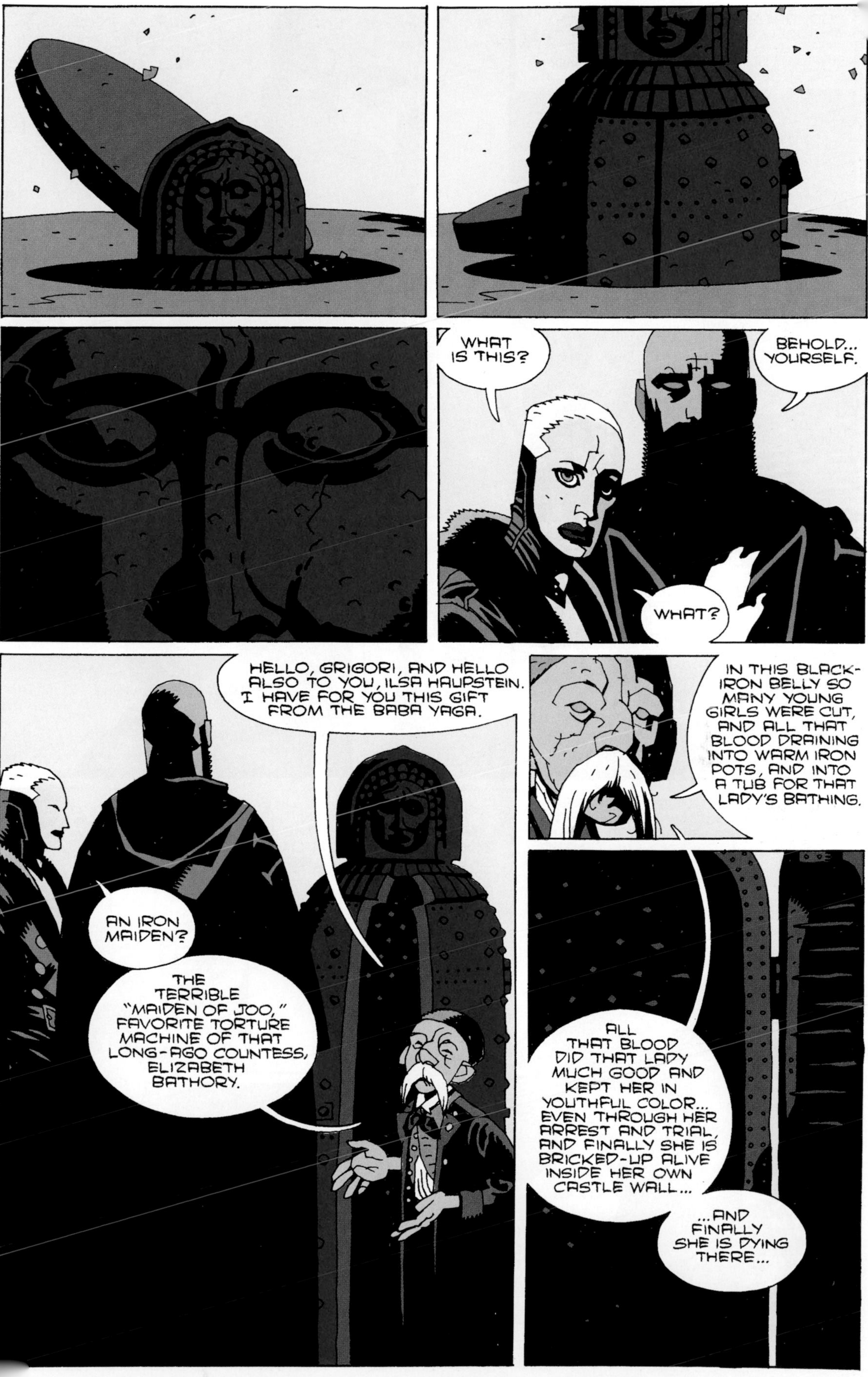
WHAT IS THIS?
BEHOLD... YOURSELF.
WHAT?
HELLO, GRIGORI, AND HELLO ALSO TO YOU, ILSA HAUPSTEIN. I HAVE FOR YOU THIS GIFT FROM THE BABA YAGA.
AN IRON MAIDEN?
THE TERRIBLE "MAIDEN OF JOO," FAVORITE TORTURE MACHINE OF THAT LONG-AGO COUNTESS, ELIZABETH BATHORY.
IN THIS BLACK-IRON BELLY SO MANY YOUNG GIRLS WERE CUT, AND ALL THAT BLOOD DRAINING INTO WARM IRON POTS, AND INTO A TUB FOR THAT LADY'S BATHING.
ALL THAT BLOOD DID THAT LADY MUCH GOOD AND KEPT HER IN YOUTHFUL COLOR... EVEN THROUGH HER ARREST AND TRIAL, AND FINALLY SHE IS BRICKED-UP ALIVE INSIDE HER OWN CASTLE WALL...
...AND FINALLY SHE IS DYING THERE...

CHAPTER FIVE

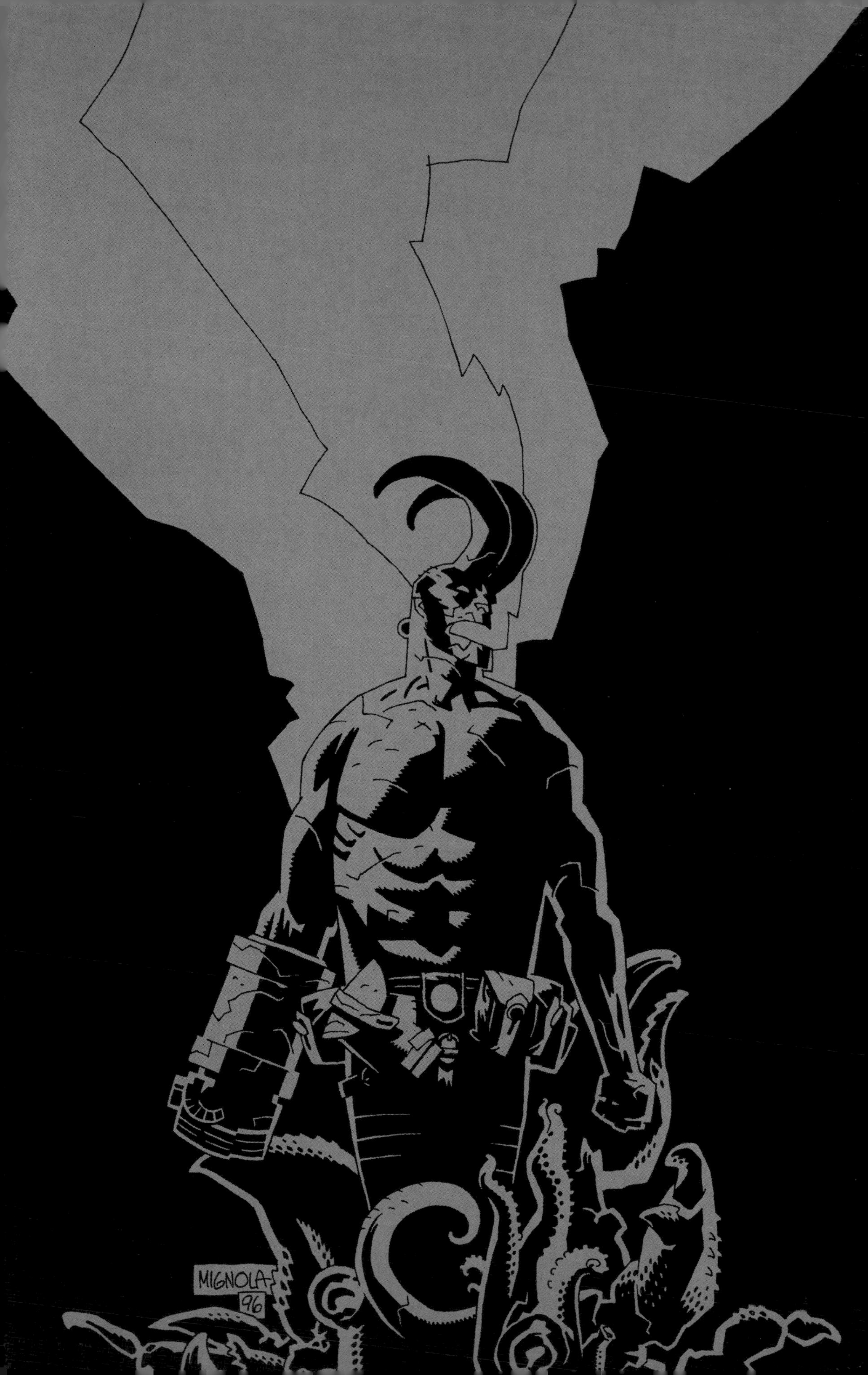
MIGNOLA
96

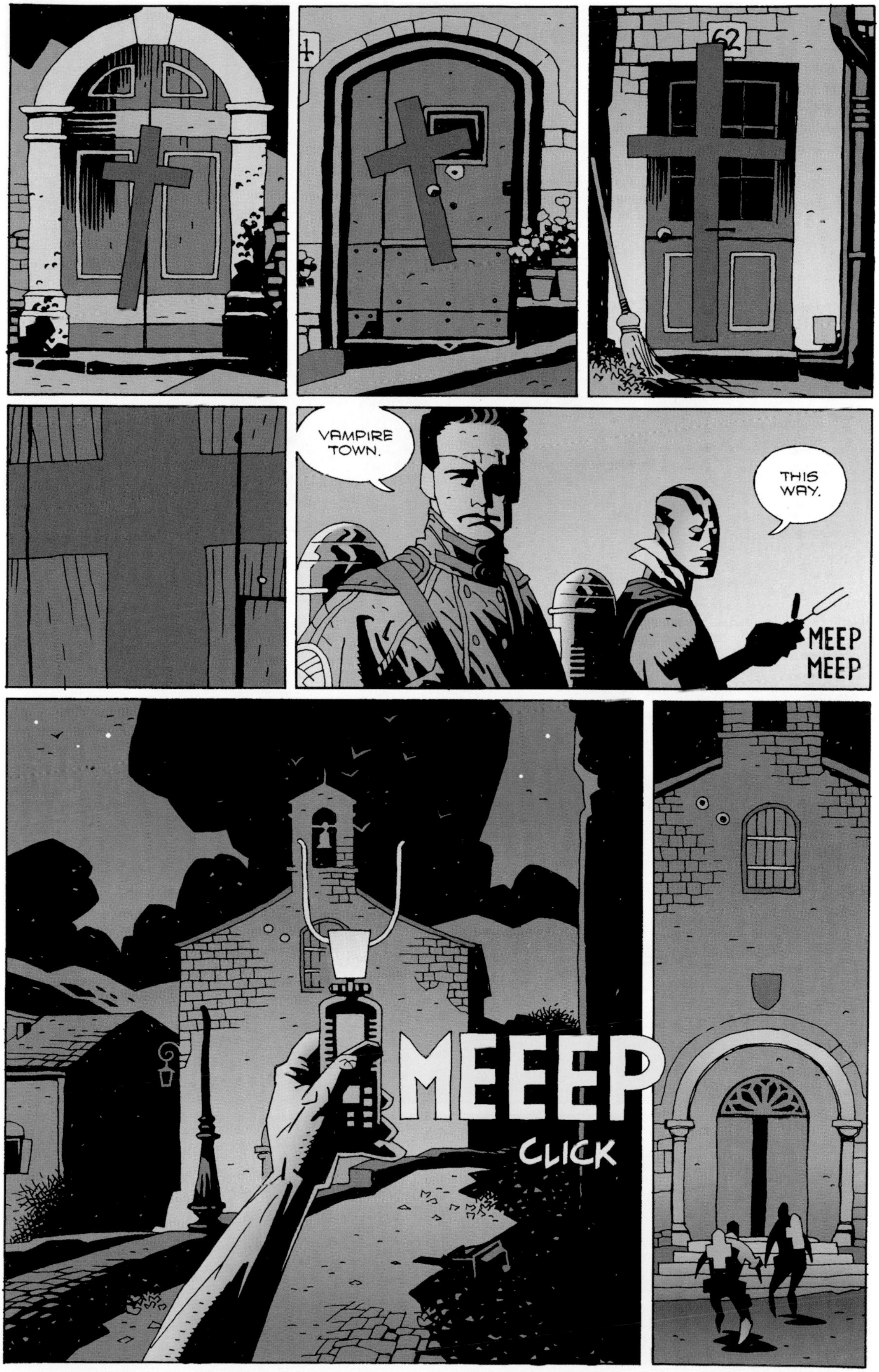
VAMPIRE TOWN.
THIS WAY.
MEEP MEEP
MEEEP
CLICK

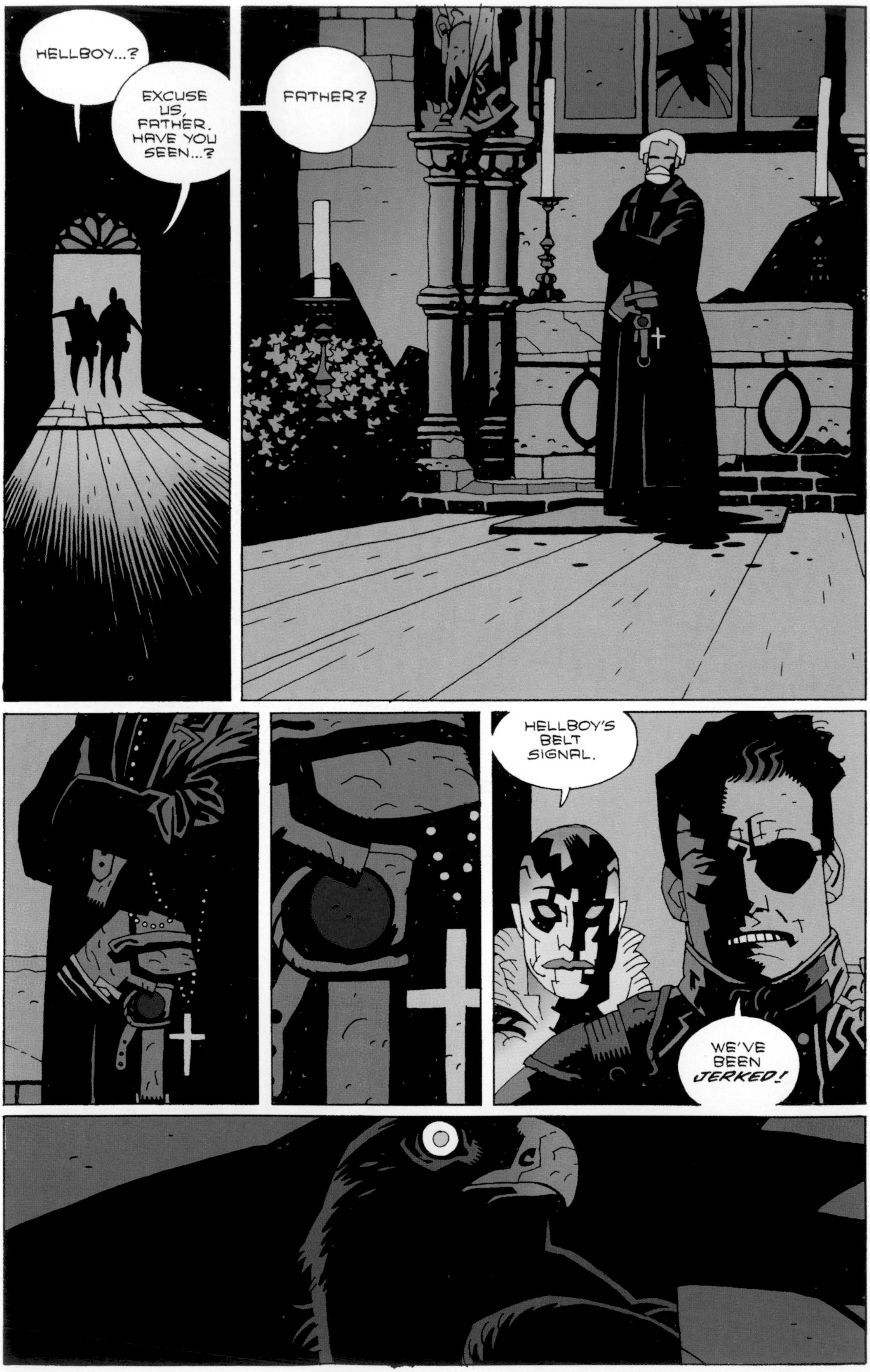
HELLBOY...?
EXCUSE US, FATHER. HAVE YOU SEEN...?
FATHER?
HELLBOY'S BELT SIGNAL.
WE'VE BEEN JERKED!

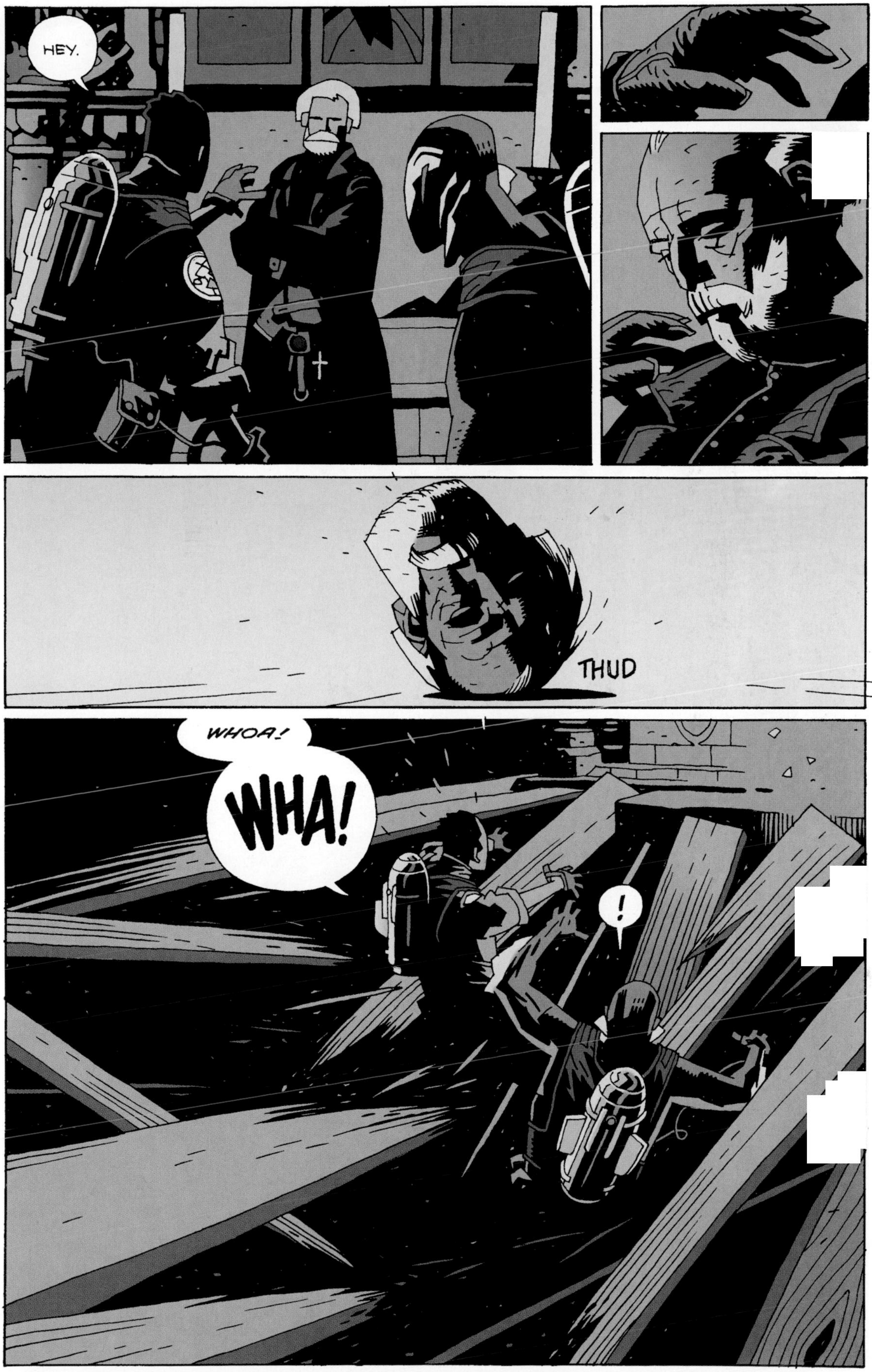
HEY.
THUD
WHOA!
WHA!
!

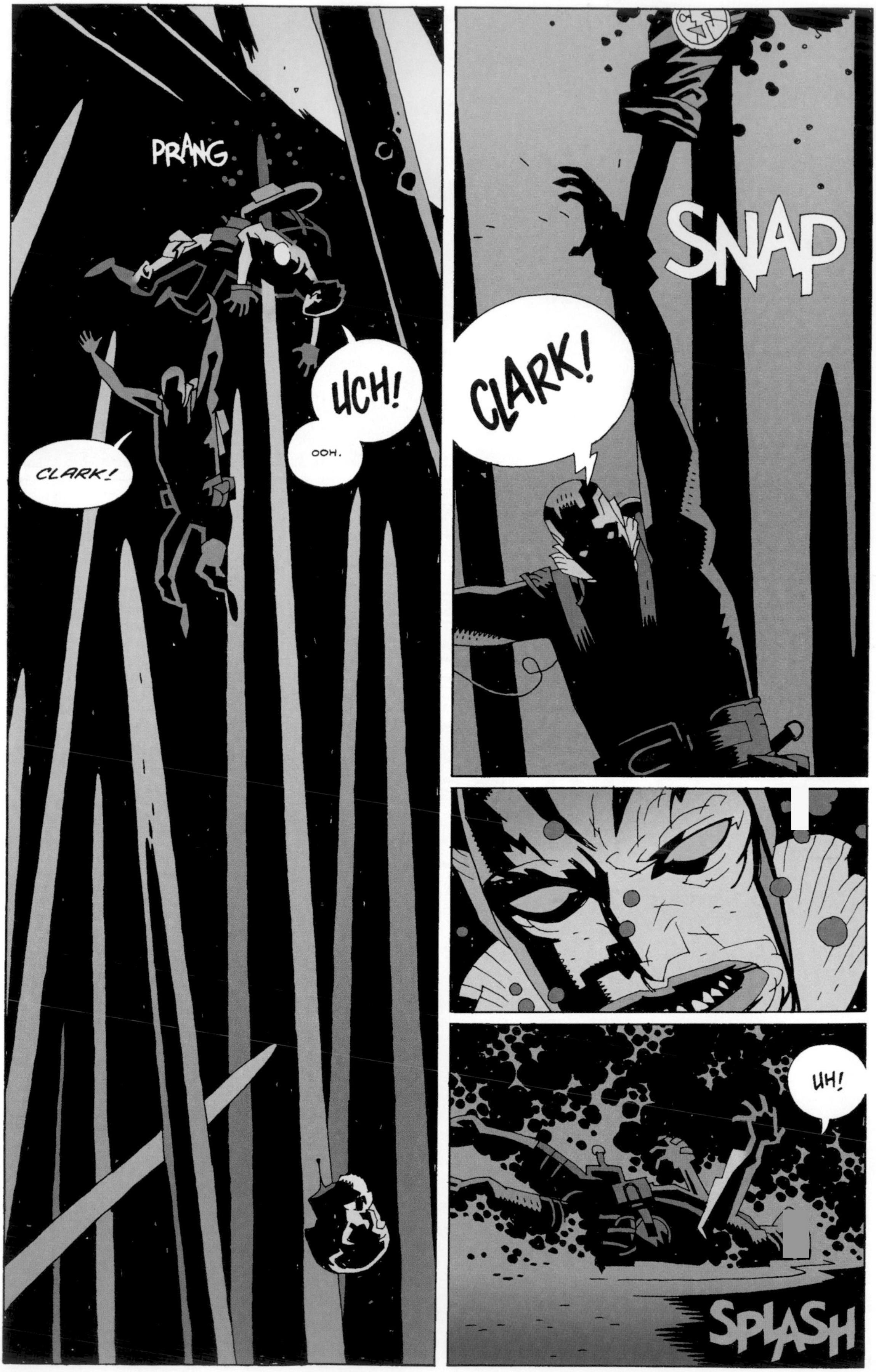
PRANG
CLARK!
UCH!
OOH.
CLARK!
SNAP
UH!
SPLASH

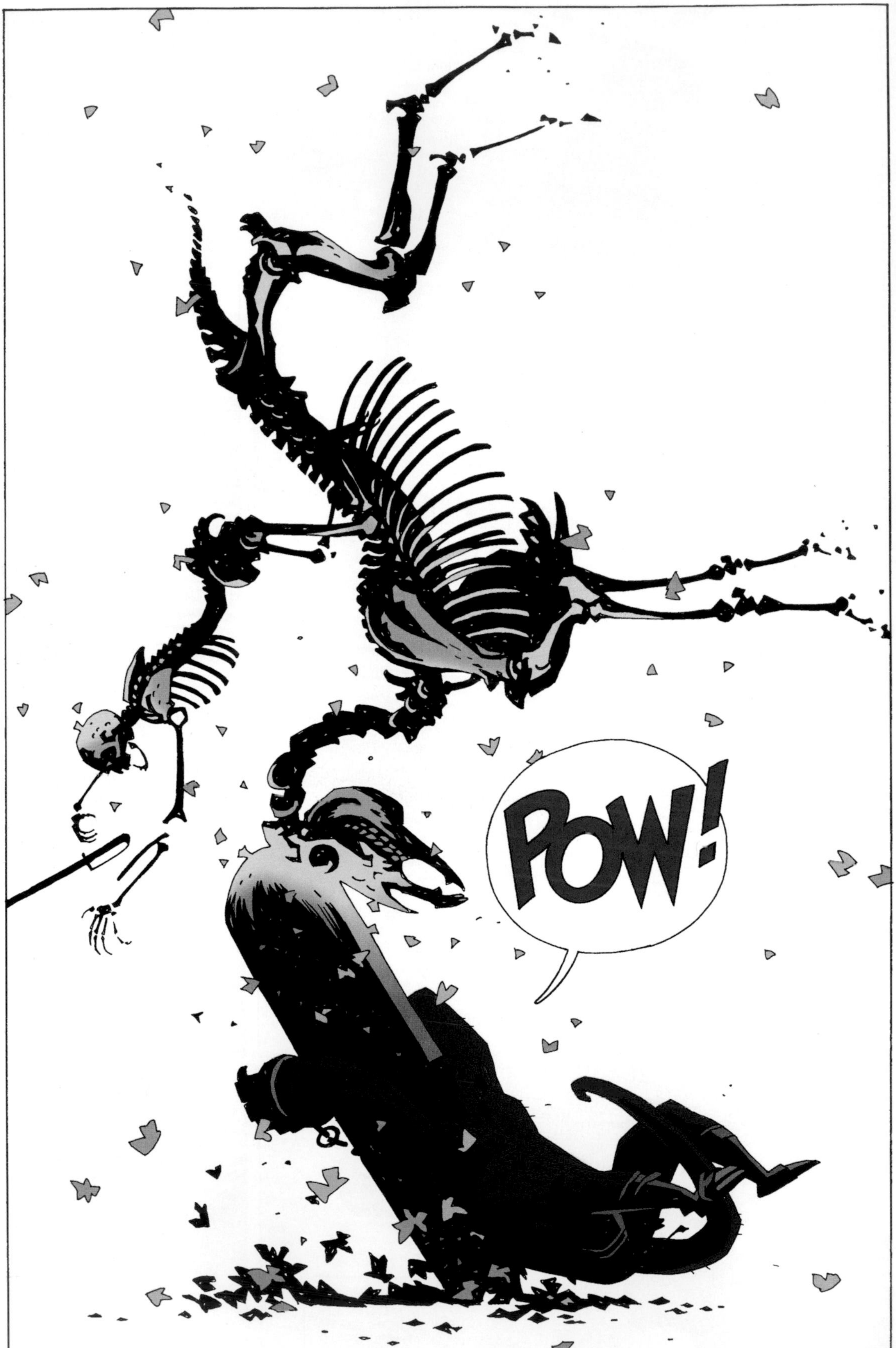
POW!

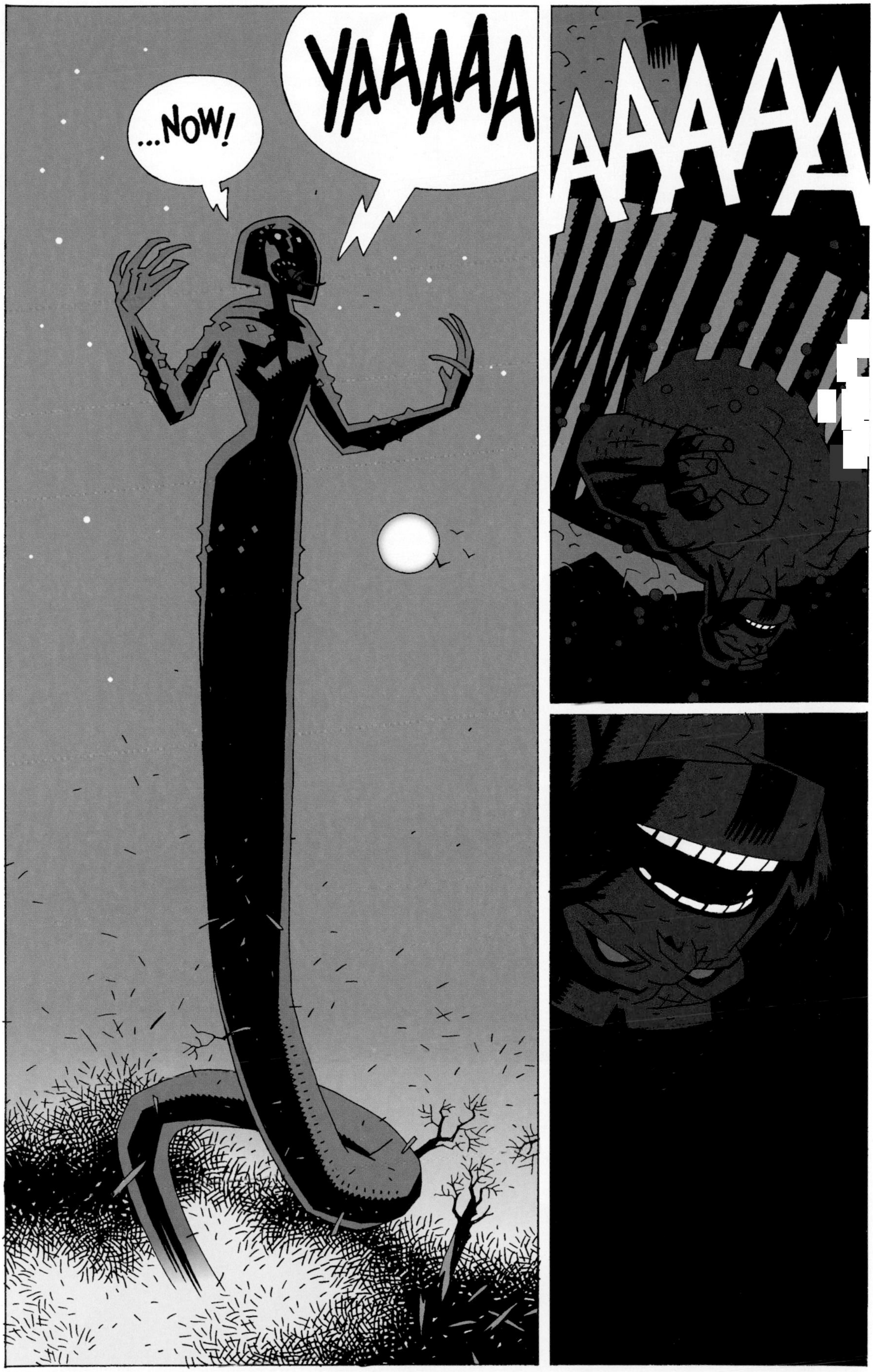
...NOW!
YAAAAA
AAAAA

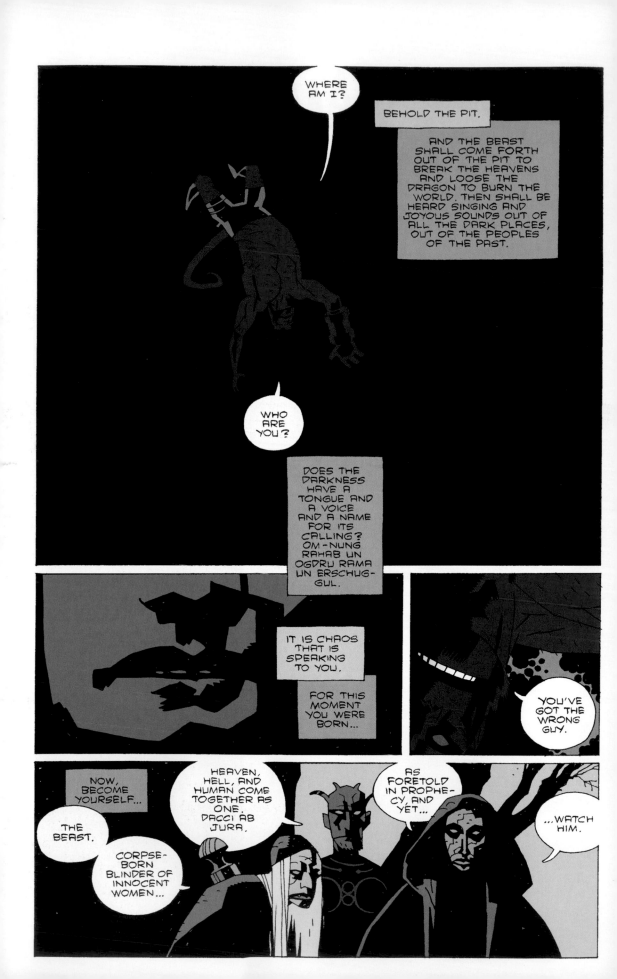

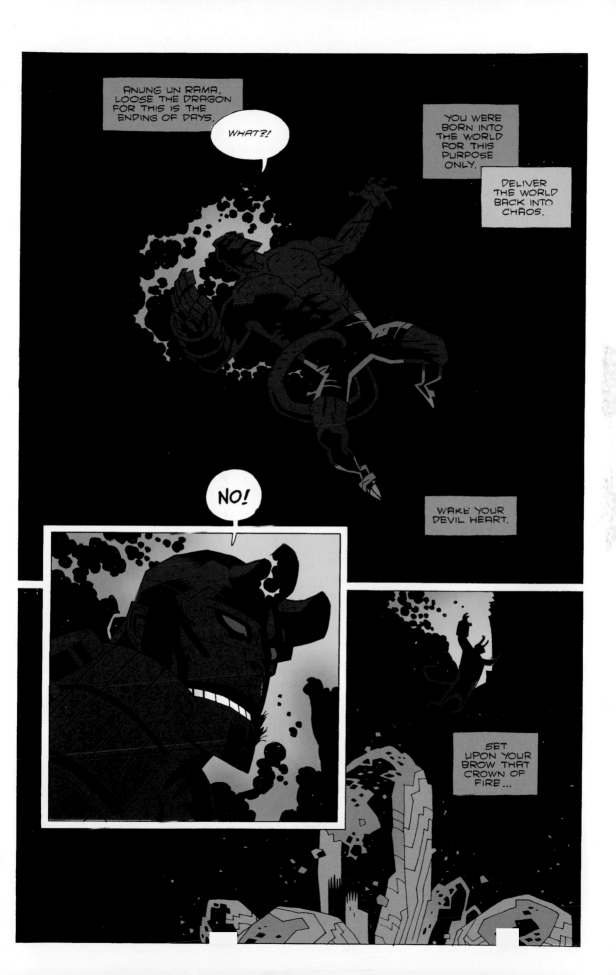

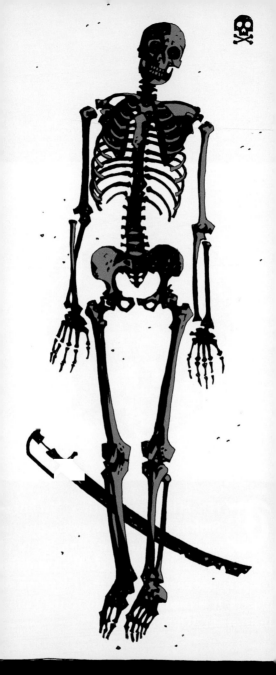

THE SKELETON of Vladimir
Giurescu was to have been moved
to BPRD headquarters in Fairfield,
Connecticut. It was placed in temporary
storage at the Bucharest airport, where it
disappeared. It has never been recovered.

T HE HEAD of Father Nicholas Budenz never spoke again, but for weeks continued to be the focus of poltergeist activities, including sudden temperature changes and the levitation of objects. It is currently on loan to the Paulvé Institute in Avignon, France.

THE BOOK YOU'RE HOLDING is the most ambitious comics project I've ever attempted as both writer and artist. When I began drawing issue one, the plot was different. The Nazis, Karl and Leopold, had a much smaller role and Herman Von Klempt, the head in a jar, wasn't in the book at all (hard to believe I would have left him out). The biggest difference was the last chapter. In the original version, Hellboy was freed from the stake at the crossroads by the Homunculus from issue three (a bit of a stretch even for me), then had a big fight to the death with Giurescu. It was okay, and probably would have worked just fine, except when I got to issue four, Hecate did all that talking about Hellboy's destiny. Well, that sort of screwed up everything. Suddenly my ending was too small. With the help of my wonderful editor (who is constantly saving me from myself), I replotted the more cosmic ending and, in the process, I think I finally made clear what those things on Hellboy's forehead are. The epilogue is brand new, done specifically for this collection.

I want to thank my wife, Christine, for putting up with me, and Scott Allie, James Sinclair, Pat Brosseau, and Cary Grazzini for making me look better than I am. Thanks to Gary Gianni for letting me run his beautiful MonsterMen story as my backup feature. Thanks to everyone who bought the comics, and a special thanks to everyone who wrote in. You've been great. You seem to want more Hellboy, so now I'm going back to work.

Goodnight.

MIKE MIGNOLA

Mike Mignola
Portland, Oregon

HELLBOY™

GALLERY

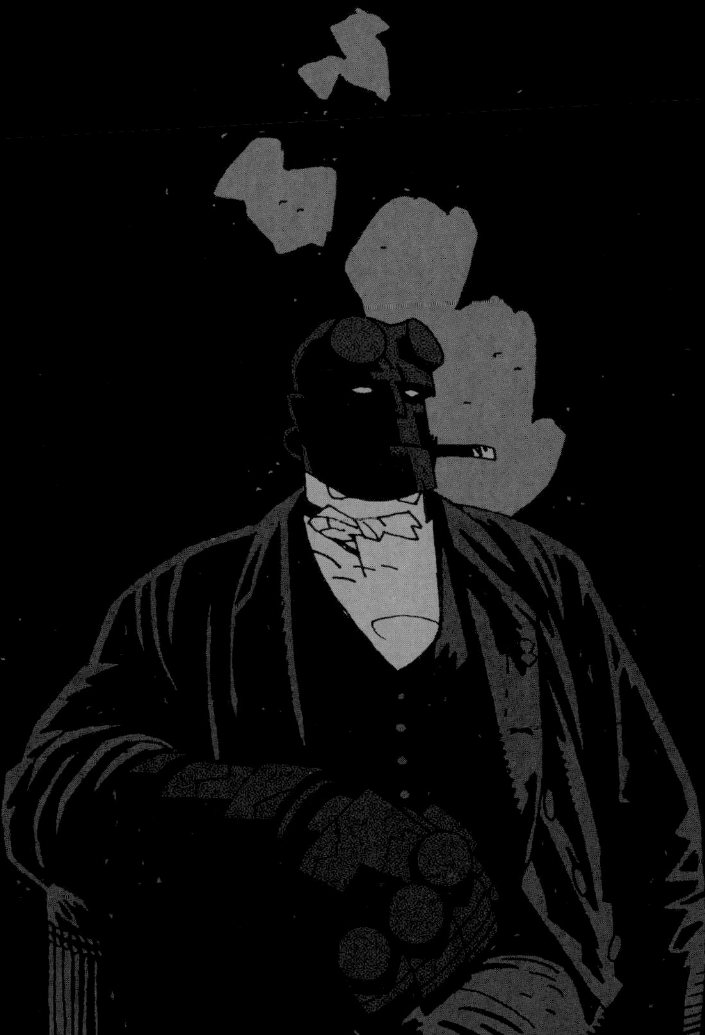

featuring

BRUCE TIMM

P. CRAIG RUSSELL

DEREK THOMPSON

DAVE COOPER

JAY STEPHENS

and

OLIVIER VATINE

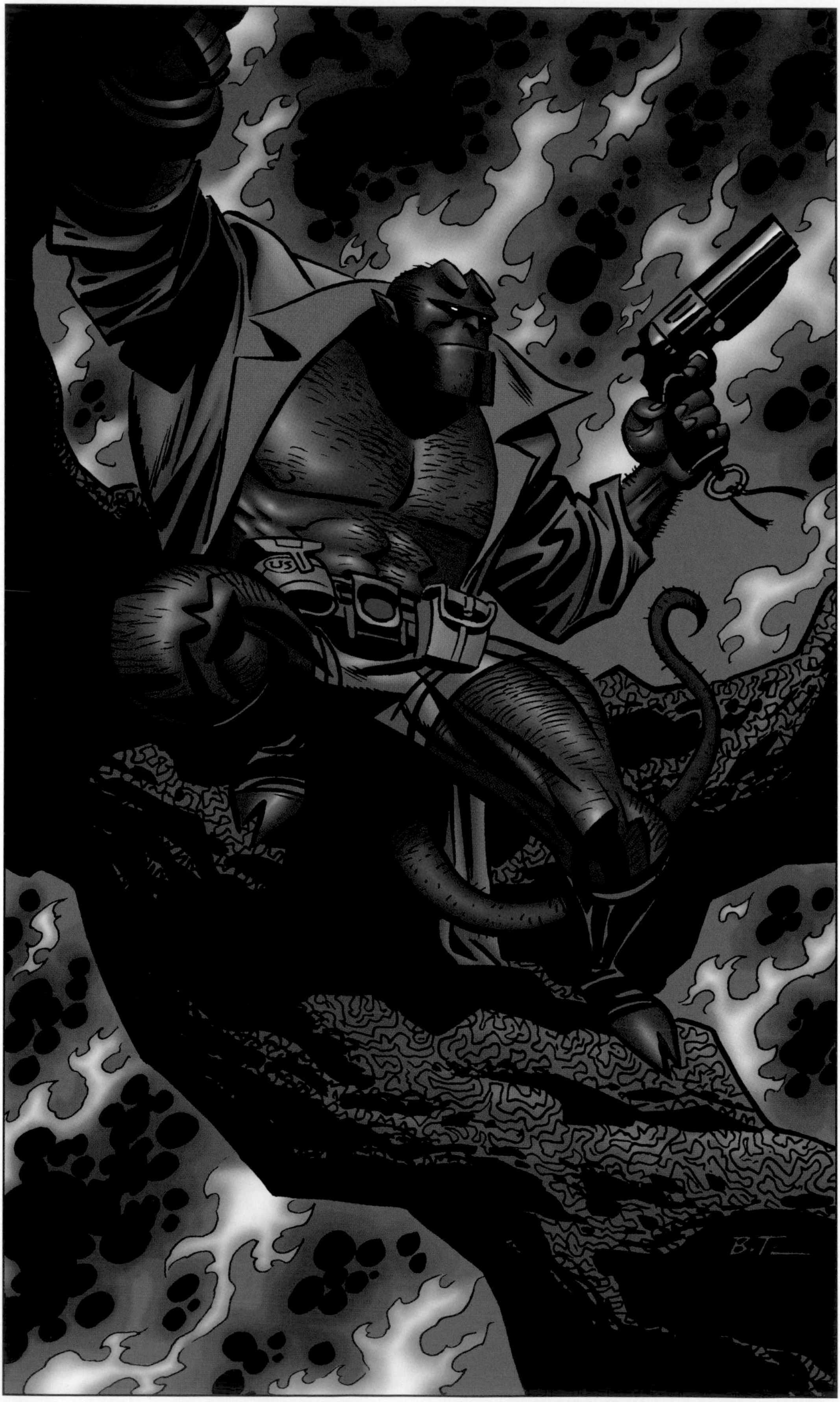

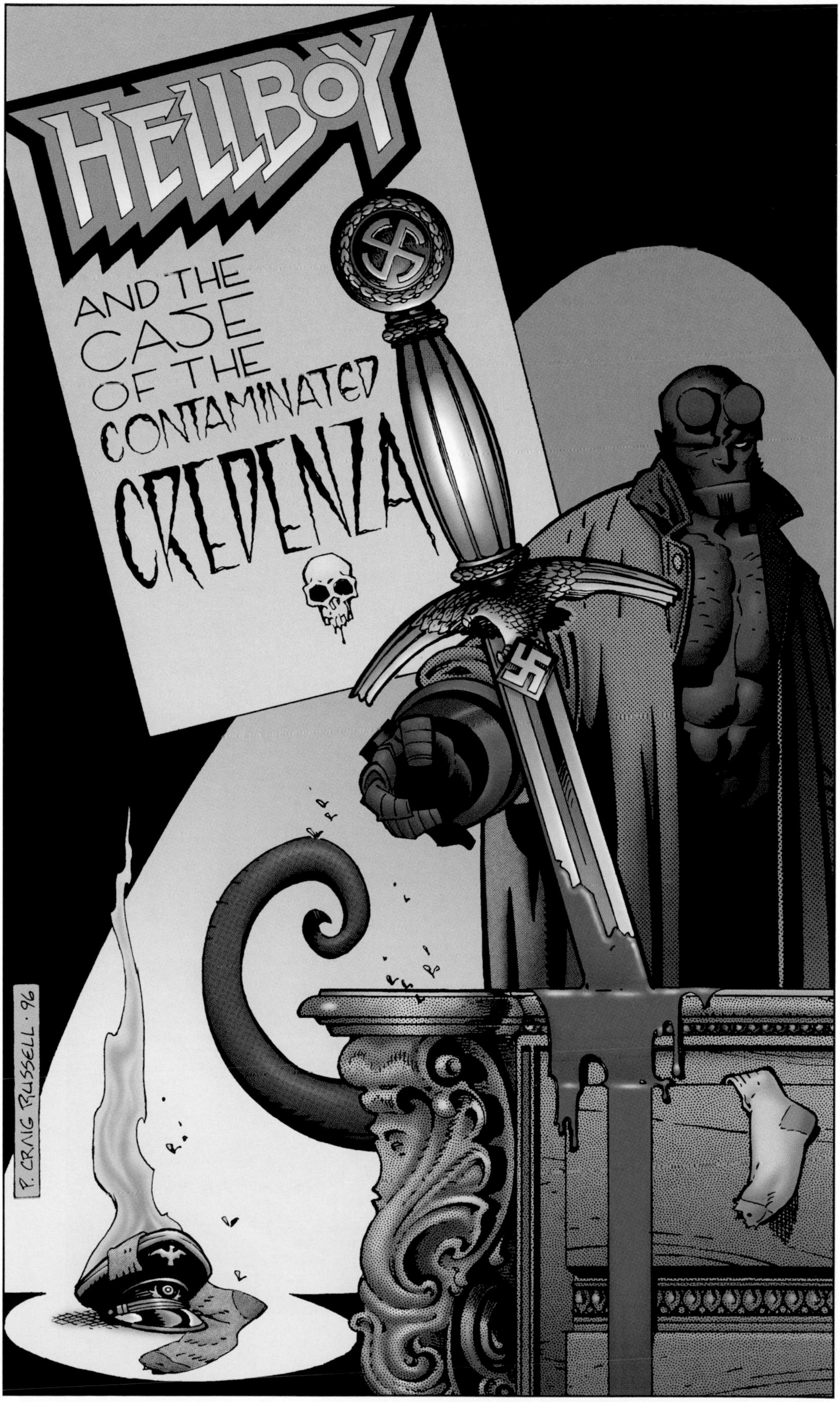
HELLBOY
AND THE CASE OF THE CONTAMINATED CREDENZA
P. CRAIG RUSSELL · 96

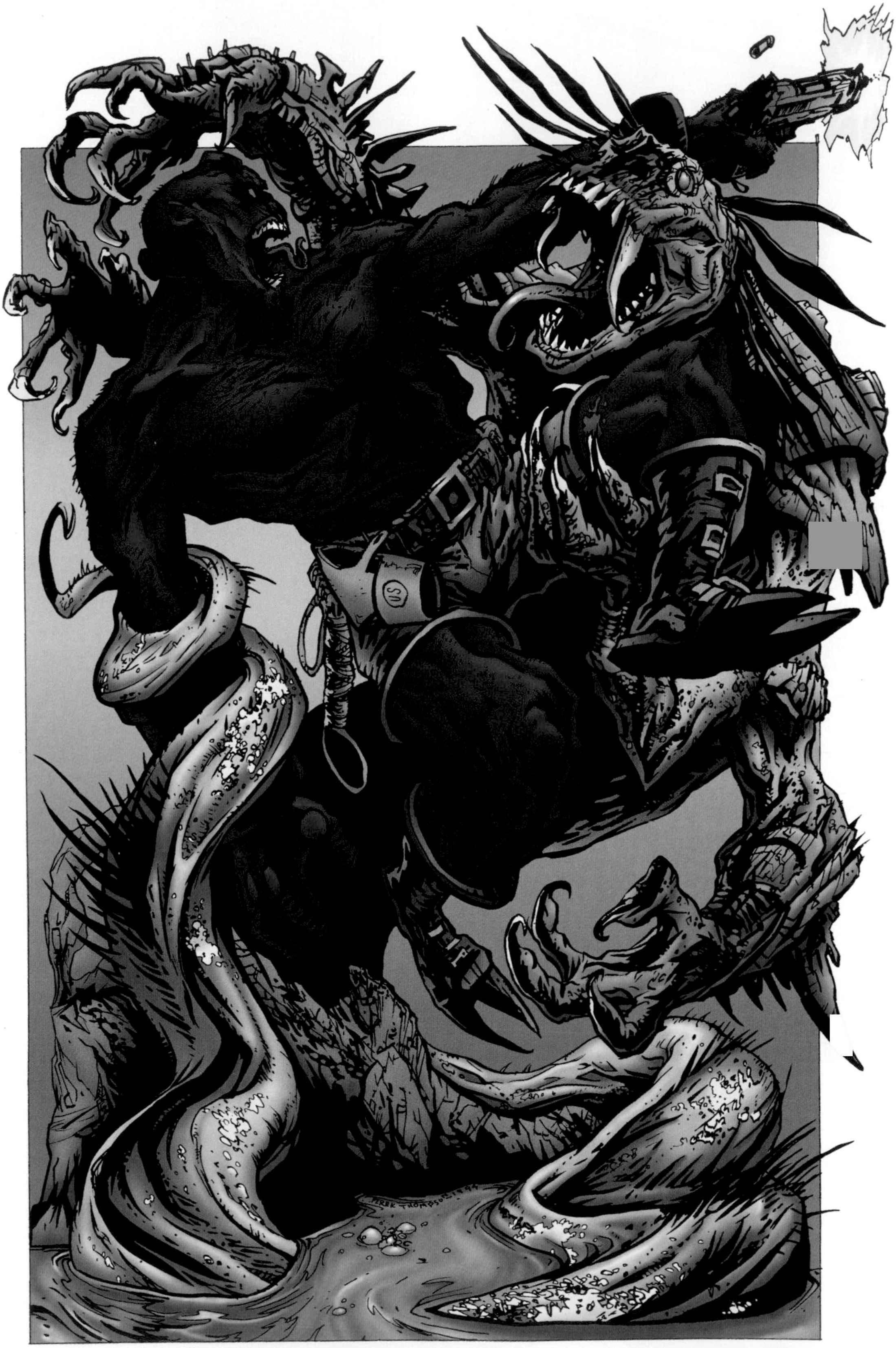

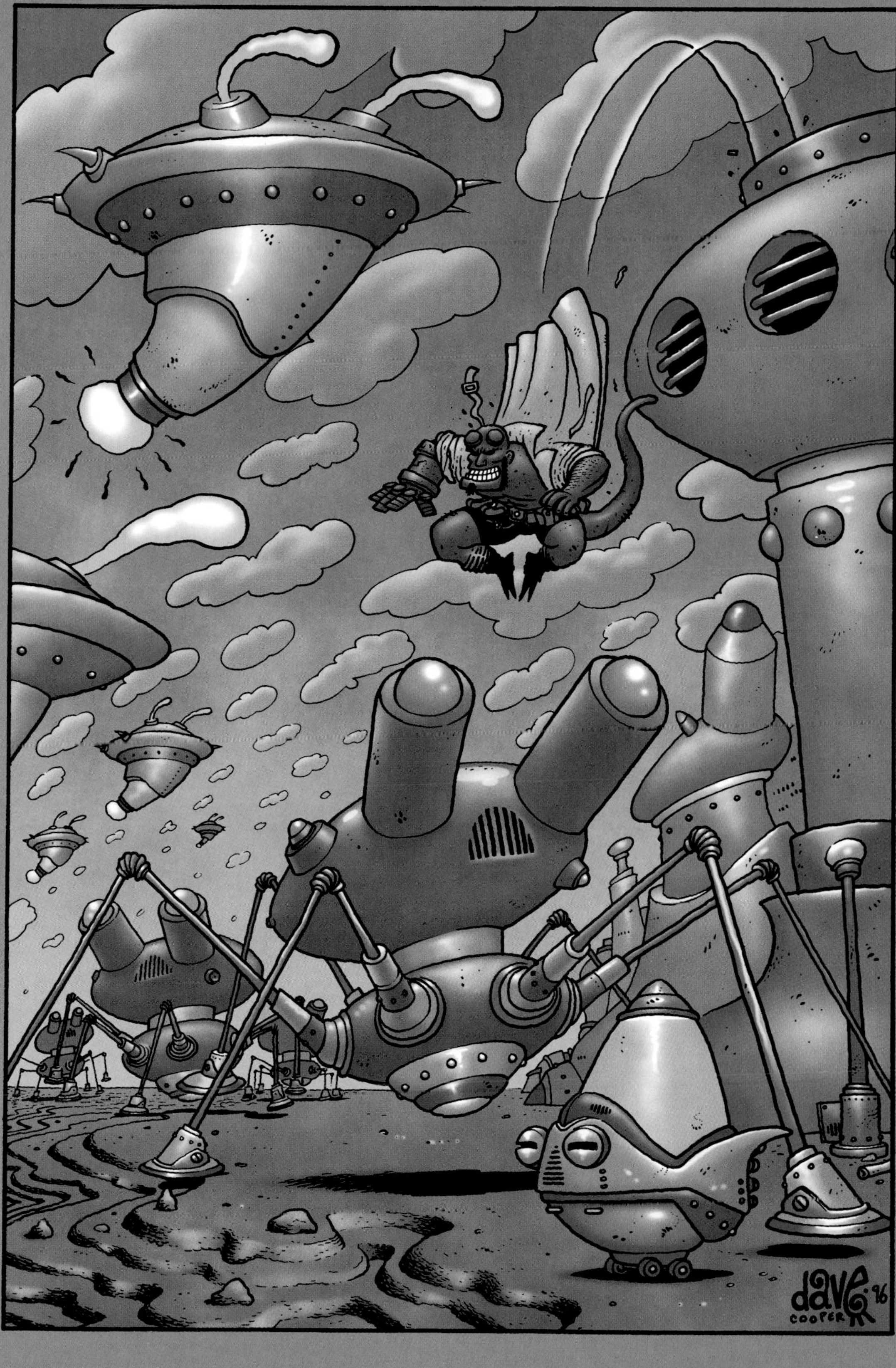
dave '96
COOPER

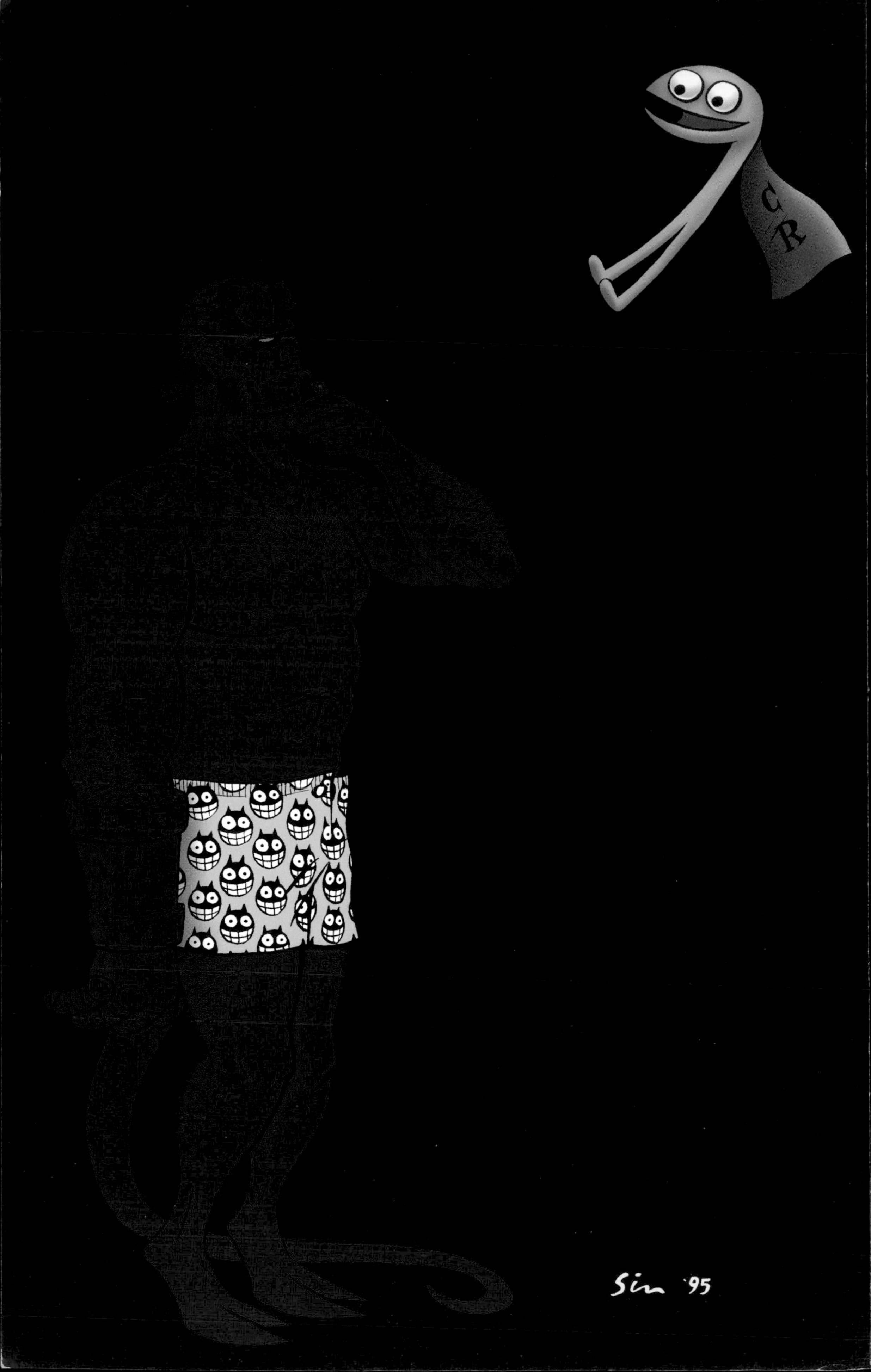
CR
Sin '95

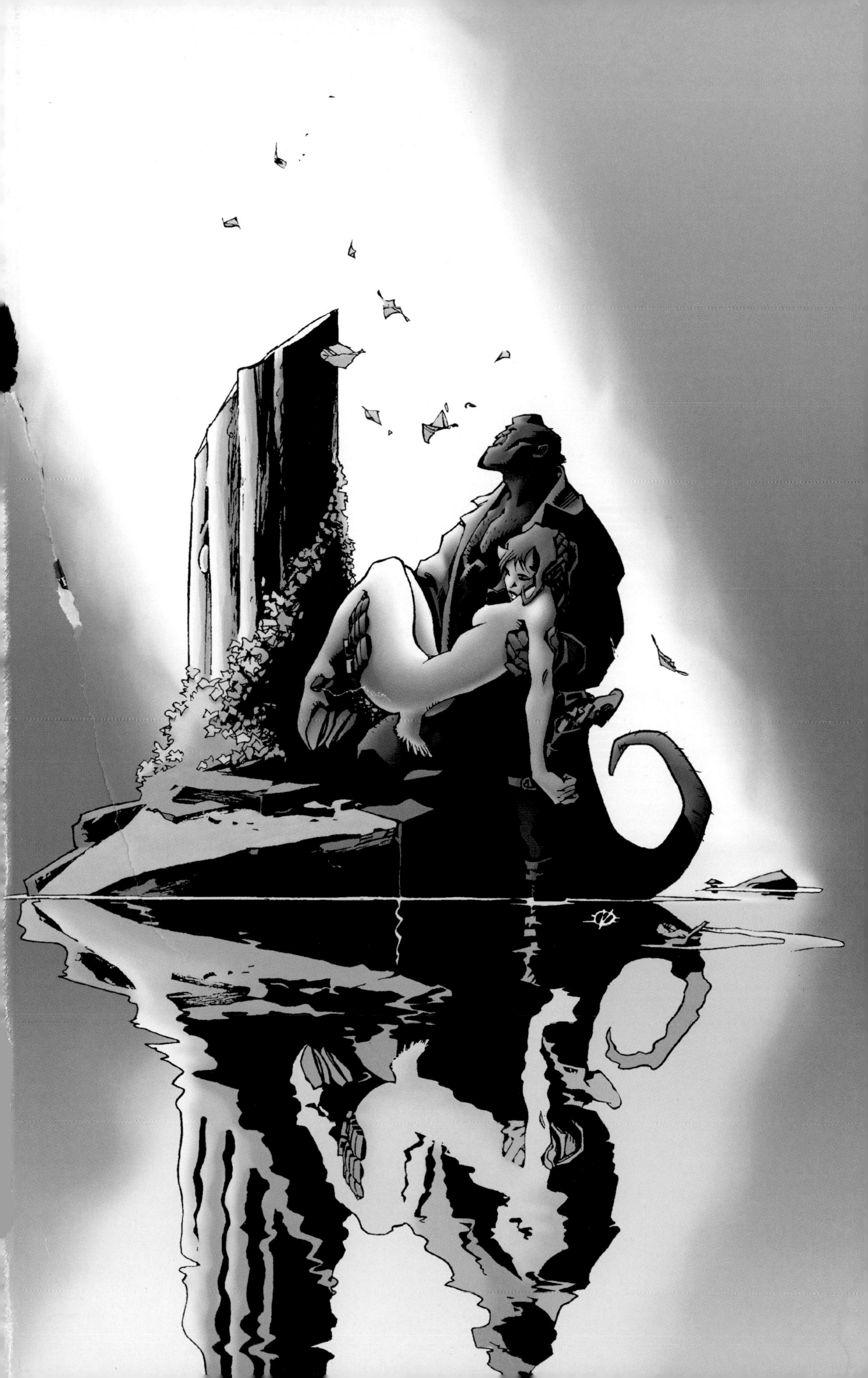

HELLBOY

by MIKE MIGNOLA

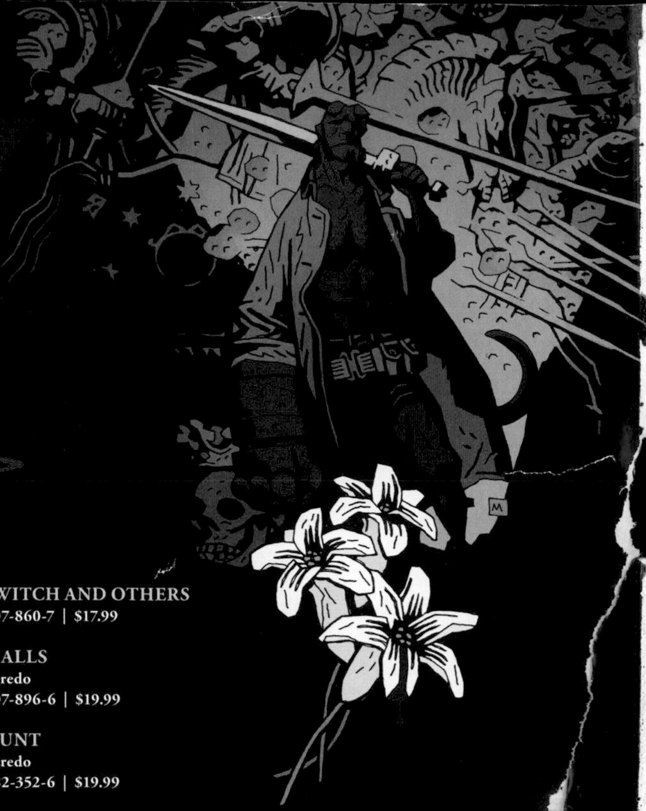

HELLBOY LIBRARY EDITION VOLUME 1:
Seed of Destruction and Wake the Devil
ISBN 978-1-59307-910-9 | $49.99

HELLBOY LIBRARY EDITION VOLUME 2:
The Chained Coffin and The Right Hand of Doom
ISBN 978-1-59307-989-5 | $49.99

HELLBOY LIBRARY EDITION VOLUME 3:
Conqueror Worm and Strange Places
ISBN 978-1-59582-352-6 | $49.99

HELLBOY LIBRARY EDITION VOLUME 4:
The Crooked Man and The Troll Witch
with Richard Corben and others
ISBN 978-1-59582-658-9 | $49.99

HELLBOY LIBRARY EDITION VOLUME 5:
Darkness Calls and the Wild Hunt
with Duncan Fegredo
ISBN 978-1-59582-886-6 | $49.99

HELLBOY LIBRARY EDITION VOLUME 6:
The Storm and the Fury and The Bride of Hell
with Duncan Fegredo, Richard Corben, Kevin Nowlan, and Scott Hampton
ISBN 978-1-61655-133-9 | $49.99

SEED OF DESTRUCTION
with John Byrne
ISBN 978-1-59307-094-6 | $17.99

WAKE THE DEVIL
ISBN 978-1-59307-095-3 | $17.99

THE CHAINED COFFIN AND OTHERS
ISBN 978-1-59307-091-5 | $17.99

THE RIGHT HAND OF DOOM
ISBN 978-1-59307-093-9 | $17.99

CONQUEROR WORM
ISBN 978-1-59307-092-2 | $17.99

STRANGE PLACES
ISBN 978-1-59307-475-3 | $17.99

THE TROLL WITCH AND OTHERS
ISBN 978-1-59307-860-7 | $17.99

DARKNESS CALLS
with Duncan Fegredo
ISBN 978-1-59307-896-6 | $19.99

THE WILD HUNT
with Duncan Fegredo
ISBN 978-1-59582-352-6 | $19.99

THE CROOKED MAN AND OTHERS
with Richard Corben
ISBN 978-1-59582-477-6 | $17.99

THE BRIDE OF HELL AND OTHERS
with Richard Corben, Kevin Nowlan, and Scott Hampton
ISBN 978-1-59582-740-1 | $19.99

HELLBOY IN HELL VOLUME 1: THE DESCENT
ISBN 978-1-61655-444-6 | $17.99

THE STORM AND THE FURY
with Duncan Fegredo
ISBN 978-1-59582-827-9 | $19.99

HOUSE OF THE LIVING DEAD
with Richard Corben
ISBN 978-1-59582-757-9 | $14.99

THE MIDNIGHT CIRCUS
with Duncan Fegredo
ISBN 978-1-61655-238-1 | $14.99

HELLBOY: THE FIRST 20 YEARS
ISBN 978-1-61655-353-1 | $19.99

THE ART OF HELLBOY
ISBN 978-1-59307-089-2 | $29.99

HELLBOY II: THE ART OF THE MOVIE
ISBN 978-1-59307-964-2 | $24.99

HELLBOY: THE COMPANION
ISBN 978-1-59307-655-9 | $14.99

HELLBOY: WEIRD TALES
VOLUME 1
ISBN 978-1-56971-622-9 | $17.99
VOLUME 2
ISBN 978-1-56971-953-4 | $17.99

HELLBOY: MASKS AND MONSTERS
with James Robinson and Scott Benefiel
ISBN 978-1-59582-567-4 | $17.99

NOVELS

HELLBOY: EMERALD HELL
By Tom Piccirilli
ISBN 978-1-59582-141-6 | $12.99

HELLBOY: THE ALL-SEEING EYE
By Mark Morris
ISBN 978-1-59582-141-6 | $12.99

HELLBOY: THE FIRE WOLVES
By Tim Lebbon
ISBN 978-1-59582-204-8 | $12.99

HELLBOY: THE ICE WOLVES
By Mark Chadbourn
ISBN 978-1-59582-205-5 | $12.99

SHORT STORIES

Illustrated by Mike Mignola

HELLBOY: ODD JOBS
By Poppy Z. Brite, Greg Rucka, and others
ISBN 978-1-56971-440-9 | $14.99

HELLBOY: ODDER JOBS
By Frank Darabont, Guillermo del Toro, and others
ISBN 978-1-59307-226-1 | $14.99

HELLBOY: ODDEST JOBS
By Joe R. Lansdale, China Miéville, and others
ISBN 978-1-59307-944-4 | $14.99

AVAILABLE AT YOUR LOCAL COMICS SHOP OR BOOKSTORE! • To find a comics shop in your area, call 1-888-266-4226.
For more information or to order direct visit DarkHorse.com or call 1-800-862-0052 Mon.–Fri. 9 AM to 5 PM Pacific Time.
Prices and availability subject to change without notice.

DARK HORSE BOOKS
DarkHorse.com